WINOLOGY™:The 48 Laws c

WINOLOGY™
The 48 Laws of Winning

by

Raymond "Big Ray" Hardy

Hardy, Raymond
WINOLOGY™: The 48 Laws of Winning

Raymond Hardy © 2017. pp. 317

ISBN-13: 978-1542372008

ISBN-10: 1542372003

1. Self-Help 2. Motivation 3. Relationships 4. Sports Psychology 5. Business Marketing 6. Finance 7. How-To 8.Spiritual

---

Copyright © 2017 by Raymond Hardy

All rights reserved. Printed in the United States of America. No part of this book may be reproduced in any manner whatsoever without the written permission, except in the case of brief quotations embedded in critical articles, and reviews. For permission to use material from this text in any form contact Raymond Hardy.

For information contact Raymond Hardy at
CHOSEN ONE SPORTS
P.O. BOX 821446
North Richland Hills, Texas 76182
(972)CHOSEN-1
Chosen1Sports@gmail.com

www.Chosen1Sports.com
www.BigRayInternational.com
www.MillionDollarSideHustle.com
***For Speaking Engagements or Bulk Orders Contact: (972)CHOSEN-1**

***Disclaimer**: The reader is responsible for their own behavior and this book is not to be considered legal or personal advice.

- **-You can Beat 50% of the People just by working hard.**
- **-You can Beat 40% more just by doing what's RIGHT!**
- **-The Last 10% is a Dog-Fight!**

"This book coupled with a willing mind + earnest enthusiasm creates an unbeatable combination!"

Quotes of Affirmation

"Every day I go to sleep as a Winner and wake up as a Champion!"

"Yea though I walk through the Valley of The Shadow of Death,

I shall fear No Evil!

Why?

Because I'm the Baddest Cat in the Jungle!

"Champions Always Find a Way to Win!"

Acknowledgements

"This work is dedicated to my Creator, to those who have created me and to those that I have helped to be "Great", in addition to those along the journey whose time may have expired but still keep me inspired. I give GOD THE GLORY and let the rest tell the story. I would like to thank the people that have helped me during my journey. Complete breakdown in **The Acknowledgements Chapter: aka "The Treasure Chapter". Page 261**

Although there are many who have contributed to my success (too many to notate or mention) I would like to give special thanks to some who have had concentrated efforts in helping me in my ascension towards greatness, because I didn't get here by myself.

Contents

Introduction

WINOLOGY™: THE 48-Laws of Winning

Winology™: 1) The study of Winning; 2) The act, theory or preparation that goes into Winning. 3) The process and preparation of putting all of the components together to produce a Winner or a Champion and come out Victorious; 4) Mastering the game of Life

*Certain aspects of this book may tend to get intense. Certain chapters will dwell on "Real-Life" experiences or may be considered PG-13. This book can help anybody but may not be for everybody because "Everybody can't Handle The TRUTH"!

"Then you will know the truth and the truth will set you free."-John 8:32

"To thine own self be true, and then you can be true to your friends!"-Shakespeare

"We are what we repeatedly do. Excellence therefore is not an act, but a HABIT!"-Aristotle

The game of Life is a gift that you received without working and/or paying for. It is structured and encompasses many levels and has simple rules to follow. *Just like there are Laws of the Jungle, Laws of Nature & Science; Laws of Gravity, there are Laws of the game of Life & Living it more abundantly. Mastering the game of Life will require time, energy, efforts and resources. The game of Life isn't going to change and neither will the outcomes unless you change your position and your mindset. To enhance your ability to achieve a Winning Lifestyle and assist you in your quest for Success to overcome obstacles and challenges in Life we have conducted & assembled a study on Winning. We present to you: ***WINOLOGY™: The 48-Laws of Winning.***

** Playing by these Laws or Rules will give you insight, "Direction & Correction". Mastering these Laws or Rules will give you the Proper Instructions for The Proper Production! Disregarding these Laws or Rules can & sometimes will have you headed for chaos, reduction, disappointment and possibly self-destruction. {*Read Colossians 2:23}*

*** Remember that everybody on the Team plays an important part. Later on in this book The Acknowledgements Chapter* ***aka "The Treasure Chapter"*** *I will introduce you to some of the people on my team that are assets and have helped me to become $uccessful and if you need assistance mention that you heard about them from the author or by reading this book and turn some of your challenges into $olutions! {If you talk to them nice & ask for the "Big-Ray $pecial" you'll be surprised at what you might get! They may be able to help you to find some $olutions to your challenges at a reduced rate.*

******Special Notes:*** **Have a set of pens {Red, Black, Green; a pad, binder or spiral notebook &*

highlighters {Yellow, Green & Blue + a voice recorder available when you read this manuscript to take notes and achieve greater results. Take your time to absorb the knowledge that it provides and don't just race or skim through the chapters because the items that you skip could hold the solutions to your challenges. To highly impact your situation, the author suggests reading this book 7-times & no less than 3-times because the first 3-times are most important acquired knowledge} & the next applied knowledge} are for reinforcement & application of the knowledge obtained. Repetition & positive application of knowledge obtained are key ingredients in learning. Some things that you read in this book will be repeated more than once so that it can manifest into your well being.

Below is a suggested pattern for reading & studying this book to achieve optimal results and a return on your investment of time, energy and resources.

"Study to show thyself approved unto God, a workman who needeth not to be ashamed, rightly dividing the word of truth"-2 Timothy 2:15

Read-React & enjoy, Read & Highlight; Read-Underline & Take Notes; Read-Revaluate & Refresh; Read & Recommend; Read & Re-Purchase/Invest for members of Your Team {so that everybody can be on the same page! Read & WRITE YOUR OWN BOOK {so that you can leave a legacy, make a difference, impact society and position yourself for future endeavors.

COLOR GUIDE

Set of pens:

*{Red *RIGHT NOW-indicates items or areas that need immediate attention; redirection or application +serious consideration for addition to your game plan.*

{Black FUTURE-indicates important concepts & ideas that you feel are important for future growth & development,

{Green VICTORY& FINANCE-indicates any items that can help you to Win, make money, improve your situation or put you in a positive position;

{Blue DISCUSSION-indicates areas that may be topics of discussion and needs revisiting; new information that needs to be researched, shared with others to help their situation or discussed in a round table format.

Highlighters

*{Yellow *PAY ATTENTION/CAUTION/POLISH UP YOUR GAME -indicates areas or items where you need immediate focus, attention & improvement.*

{Green GO-indicates any items that motivates you, gets you in gear, inspires you to greatness or that can help you to accomplish the task at hand.

{Light-Blue SPECIAL INTEREST ITEMS-indicates

items or areas that have special meaning, sentimental value or align with your cause or Vision;

{Orange ALERT-indicates items or areas that may be of "High-Concern", "Time-Sensitive", need "Discretion" or where Decisions have to be made to avoid consequences & Repercussions or where "Life-Lessons" may have been learned {& that you don't want repeated}.

==================================
=================

WINOLOGY™: THE 48-LAWS OF WINNING

"Everybody wants to win, but doesn't want to ***"Do what it takes to Win!"-Big Ray.***

"If you want to be Great, You must do something Extra"-Percy Duhe.

"You are what you repeatedly do. Excellence therefore is not an act, but a habit"-Aristotle

"If your livelihood was contingent upon the product and/or the effort that you put forth in your industry or on the court/ field of play, what would you do different?"-Big Ray

Attitude determines Altitude, Latitude & Longitude! ***If you do what everybody else is doing, you will get everybody else's results.*** If you want different results, you must do something ***Different***. One of the definitions of Insanity is doing the same thing over and over but yet expecting a different result.

*"**Faith without works is dead**"-James 2:14-26.*

The 48-Laws of Winning are not meant to be an "*overnight sensation.*" It's a Process. It is about concepts and ideas including short-term, mid-range & long-term goal setting that make sense and will help you to make sensible choices using the resources & connections that you have to get what you want. As with any proven Success System, it will work if you work it. Don't think that because you bought this book and it looks pretty on your bookshelf that some magical fairy is going to come and put a ***Championship Ring & Trophy*** or a ***Million dollar*** **contract** under you pillow. You have to read the book (*over & over*) then apply the concepts and ideas to produce a positive mindset and flow of new ideas outside of the box there by creating alternative ways to win that can provide additional options as well as opportunities for you & your family. ***www.MillionDollarSideHustle.com***

One thing about opportunities not taken advantage of is that they don't just go away, they go to someone else. You want to put yourself into a position of being able and ready to Win.

*Before you even begin to fathom a "*Winning Lifestyle*" take an inventory of all that you have; those around you including those that you associate with. Next, visualize yourself starting/owning a multi-faceted conglomerate from the ground floor or from "scratch" if you will? Now as you transform your mind & mindset into "*Game-mode or Grind mode*" as you prepare to enter into this realm of a "*Winning Lifestyle*" imagine that you are starting a Pro Sports Franchise **PROS GET PAID**, *Amateurs don't! You* need to create several teams within the Team: Offense, Defense, Special-Teams, Administration, Support Staff, Marketing & Promotions, Concessions & Apparel, Personnel, Scouting, Finance, Security, Parking Lot Attendants & Valet, VIP-Services, Sales staff, so on & so forth.

Now categorize the people that you have taken inventory of and put them in one of the 3-following categories: **CAN HELP ME;** *CAN'T* ***HELP ME;*** **FAN IN THE STANDS!**

**{If they can help you tell them to come on; If they can't help you tell them to "Get-On"& go about their business or get them some business in their area of expertise; If they are a Fan in the Stands, tell them to buy a ticket, get in the stands and wait for the show to begin!}*

Marinate on this for a day before reading the remainder of this book because ***you are going to have to do something different in order to get different results and one of the first things is adjusting your atmosphere & associations to facilitate a positive mental attitude in addition to an environment conducive to Winning!*** The definition of insanity is "*doing the same thing over & over but yet expecting different results*" ***Always remember that with one good idea you can eat off of it for about 10 years! With 1-Great Idea you can eat off of it for a Lifetime!*** *"You were made to Prosper"!* Now get to Brainstorming!

"***You can win if you put your mind to it!*** *You just haven't figured out how-to yet"-Big-Ray*

Chapter 1
***_KEEP GOD FIRST, Because HE'S GOING TO BE FIRST_ ANYWAY**!

"Seek ye first the kingdom of GOD and his righteousness and all these things shall be added unto you"-Mathew 6:33

"Trust in the Lord with all your heart and lean not unto your own understanding"-Proverbs 3:5

"Commit to the Lord whatever you do and Your Plans will Succeed"-Proverbs 16:3 NIV

Divine connection is your access to success.

"We are all Winners through Christ Jesus who strengthens us" -Philippians 4:13

"You have to Believe to Receive!"-Big Ray

"Without faith it is impossible to please God"-Hebrews 11:6.

***YOUR RELATIONSHIP WITH GOD IS ESSENTIAL TO YOUR SUCCESS!**

When you surrender to GOD, that's when you can get ready to be blessed by GOD! Ask GOD to change your mindset so that you can be able to receive. He said in his word:

"That I wish above all things that you prosper and be in good health even as your soul prospers"-3John 1:2

To be able to accomplish anything in life, one must first be able to: Conceive, Believe And Receive that the accomplishment can happen, will happen and is destined to happen! The CBAR concept was developed by legendary Coach & noted speaker Ray Hardy. In the sports world, they taught us an important concept to *"Always take care of home"!* Home is where the heart is, in addition to where your Family & most precious items are.

The only reason men fail is due to broken focus. You must target that of which you desire the most and pursue it relentlessly.

"A man must have a job! A job is what's necessary!"-Coach Cunningham

Chapter 2
A WINNER IS NOT A QUITTER AND A QUITTER IS NOT A WINNER!

A "Winner" is described as someone that wins especially a victor in sports or a notably successful person".-Webster's Dictionary

*"**90% of most** Businesses **failed because they quit or they had no** marketing **plan.**"-Armani Valentino*

"80% of your success is going to be achieved by you showing up and being busy."-Armani Valentino

Winning is about Achievement. In order to win, be successful or be victorious you have to complete your tasks, assignments or competitions preferably before or better than the competition. It also helps if you have your mindset in the proper mode or at the proper confidence level to win or complete assignments so that you can get accustomed to achieving things on a consistent basis.

"***The game is 90% mental***"!

- *"You Beat 50% of the people just by working hard"!*
- *"You Beat 40% more by doing what's right"!*
- *The Last 10% is a dog-fight"!*

Most people enter into competitions or business agreements "***thinking***" that they only have a 50-50 or a 50% chance of being victorious or successful in their outcomes. The Bible has a parable that makes reference to: *"...So as a man thinketh in his heart, so is he".* Some Scientist say that most people use only 10% of their brain. If we utilized our brains just a fraction more & entered into situations thinking that we would win, we would come out victorious more often than with the previous thought pattern of a 50-50 win percentage.

Whenever you enter into a competition or accept an assignment or task always do it well or to the "*Best*" of your ability and make sure that you "*Complete*" the assignment or task at hand. Reasons being is that you are always being watched & evaluated and as you go through Life you develop a track record. Your "*performance & productivity*" is not only a reflection of you, your team or company that you represent, but more so of the GOD that you serve.

"We can do all things through Christ Jesus who strengthens us".

There will be times in life where it's not always about coming in first but more so about crossing the finish line. All things in life are not always a "*Sprint*", sometimes it comes in the form of a "*Marathon or a Journey*" and finishing the race. So whenever you approach a task or an assignment, do it as if you are doing it for GOD.

Anticipate and avoid unnecessary conflicts in addition to never entering into a battle, contest or war where there is no reward.

- 10% of most conflict or confusion comes from a difference of opinion or philosophy. The other 90% comes from using the wrong tone of voice.

Chapter 3
FAITH: YOU HAVE TO BELIEVE TO RECEIVE!

"Faith is the substance of thing hoped for and evidence of things not yet seen"-Hebrews 11:1

"I can do all things through Christ who strengthens me"-Philippians 4:13

To be able to accomplish anything in life, one must first be able to: Conceive, Believe And Receive that the accomplishment can happen, will happen and is destined to happen! The CBAR concept was developed by legendary Coach & noted speaker Ray Hardy.

Anything that you can encompass with your 5-senses can be obtained. *{If you can Think it, see it, smell it, taste it, hear it or touch it, "It" can be Yours!}*

- ***Before beginning this process of adjusting your belief system, ask yourself these questions to eliminate "Time-wasting":***
    - ***#1) How bad do you want "It" or need "It"?***
    - ***#2) Are you willing to do what it takes to obtain "It"?***
    - ***#3) Are you willing to do what it takes to maintain 'It" once "It" is obtained?***

It is your Belief System and your mindset that is going to help you to overcome obstacles and adversity to become Victorious. A lot of people in the Sports world set out to become one the best players to play the game. We position the people under our tutelage to visualize being not only one of the best players in the game, but to be one of the best owners in the game. Instead of just trying to be Jerry Rice, consider being a Jerry Jones, a Jerry Buss or a Mark Cuban. ***Playing the game has eligibility factors and/ or an expiration date***. Regardless of whether you are playing, coaching or in an administrative capacity, you want to take ownership of your situation. When you take ownership of a situation, it puts your mind in a position of dominance over your domain, position or property. When I played ball, I owned my position and was one of the Best at what I did. It wasn't any sharing, swapping out or rotating at my position. If someone came in that played my position, they had to learn how to play something else.

Another example is that when you were younger, it might have been somebody in the neighborhood who could have gotten the best of you out in the community, but if they were over your house or in your yard, they had to abide by your rules or leave. When you were at home, your mindset was more in a position of dominance & lacking of fear. This is why a lot of Coaches stress "***We must Protect this House***" when hosting Home games or events to put their player's mindset in a mode of domination or protect mode. An analogy that I used to employ was that "*If somebody over 6'4, 300lbs tried to break* *you're your house, come through the window & do something dastardly to your Mother and Little Sister, what are you going to do? Are you going to "Man-Up" and go into "Attack-mode" or tuck tail like a coward and run out of the back door? I then go into a spiel about cutting them off at the point of attack like we teach in sports and shut the window down on their neck like a guillotine or grab that poker stick off of the fireplace and beat that head & beat that head some more until that behind lays down!* When you change your mindset to a different mode of operations, you get different results. Ownership most times puts you more in control of your destiny, lasts longer and gives you more options to decide when and how to get out.

Next, scientists say that humans only use 10% of their brain. **Imagine how much more productive that you could be if you would just take a moment to "*Think*" and utilize your brain more often.** The word *"Think"* (which is an action word that's underutilized) can actually be used to stimulate & motivate your mind to create better opportunities to elevate you out of your present situation instead of regular *"stinking-thinking"* of being boxed in. Does the term *"Thinking outside of the box"* ring a bell? If you change your way of thinking, you can change your outcome or results. The Bible says that

"So as a man thinketh in his heart, so is he."-Proverbs 23:7

The key question is whose report do you believe? Are you going to listen to the *"naysayer"* or the people who are telling you that it can't be done or are you going to follow what's in your heart and find a way to win? Start thinking Great things & Greatness will draw to you. If you subscribe to a losing attitude, you will accumulate losses. You can decide your own destiny based on the level of your *"Desire, Dedication & Determination" aka"The 3-D's".* ***If you would just take the time to "Think" of 10-12 new things daily that you can do to improve your situation & implement them into your game plan over the next 21-40 days, watch & document the turnaround as your improvements transform into habits and later transitions into a Lifestyle.*** To assist you with this transition, I am going to plant some *"Seeds of Faith"* with you and give you a few nuggets of *"Wisdom"* to marinate on as you continue on this journey towards *"Greatness".* *"Thinking"* is a discipline and so is *"Studying".*

"Faith comes by hearing & hearing the word of GOD"

****Special Note:** ***We will touch upon Discipline & Studying a little more in Chapter 8 as well as expound more on components of Faith in other chapters including***

Ch. 5 Study to Show Thyself Approved; Ch. 10 If you want to be Great, Surround Yourself with Greatness; Ch. 21 IF YOU WANT DIFFERENT RESULTS, DO SOMETHING DIFFERENT; &Ch. 42 Always have a Game Plan at Hand.;

Chapter 4
KNOW WHAT GAME YOU'RE PLAYING BEFORE YOU COMPETE

"If you can't win, don't Loose"!-Big-Ray

"Do not enter a war without knowing your going to Win"!-Mike Murdock

"The most important thing to remember if you want to win a dog fight is to make sure that you bring the right dog"-Yusef L.Chew

"There are no office hours for Champions" Paul Dietzel

Know what a Winner is & What it takes to Win before you begin! Understand How the System Works. Have a thorough understanding of any contest, event, situation or circumstance that you are contemplating getting involved in or with in addition to knowing the Rules, regulations, goals & aspirations of such including the anticipated rewards of coming out victorious or consequences & repercussions of failing to do so.

"Wisdom is the principal thing; therefore get wisdom and with all thy getting, get understanding"-Proverbs 4:7

Anticipate and avoid unnecessary conflicts in addition to never entering into a battle, contest or war where there is no reward.

Chapter 5
STUDY TO SHOW THYSELF APPROVED

"Study to show thyself approved unto God, a workman who needeth not to be ashamed, rightly dividing the word of truth"-2 Timothy 2:15

"Write The Things Which Thou Hast Seen, And The Things Which are, And The Things Which Shall Be Hereafter."-Revelation 1:19

"67% of most people that graduate from college never open or read another book in their life." Dr. George C. Fraser

To master the game, you must first become a student of the game.

"Whatever you want to become, whatever you want to achieve or acquire they have a book on it."-Big-Ray

Readers are Leaders and the reason why is because most of them are ahead of the game in reference to knowledge & application of that knowledge.

The Bible says that *"my people perish for a lack of knowledge..."-Hosea 4:6. {some translations state "are destroyed" instead of "perish".*

This passage hold true in various facets of life: Spiritual, Social, Physical, Financial, Business and Relationships.

To Win Consistently you should have knowledge of your Game and constantly be on top of you Game**.** **Life is a never ending *"learning experience"*** with new techniques, procedures and plays being developed every day**. Don't let anything distract you from gaining the knowledge you need to be successful.** *Never get complacent because you've experienced some symbolism of success.* **Stay focused and sharp because the day you lay off is the day it won't pay off.** You must become a student/scholar of the game before you Master it. **After you Master the Game, you then want to take Ownership.**

In the Sports world, we study film so that we can find our mistakes, correct our actions and then eliminate the mistakes. In both Sports & the Business and financial industry, we study & monitor stats, numbers & productivity to determine which areas are deficient, need attention or reduction, in addition to the areas that will bring abundant increase & profitability.

Sometimes in the game of life, you don't get that opportunity to roll back the film or the clock to correct your mistakes, so it's best to be on top of your game and minimize the possibility of mistakes before you leave the house, because it's a jungle out there. Everybody in the jungle has an agenda, a job, objective or a purpose when they wake up. When the Deer, the Antelope & the Wilder beast wake up every day and leave the house, their objective is not to get eaten alive and return home safely. When the Lions, Tigers, Jaguars & Leopards leave the house every day, their objective is to obtain something to eat and bring it back home to feed their family. Until you can develop your game or position yourself to where you are no longer the hunted, you have to take precautionary measures to survive in this game called *"Life".*

"Self-Preservation is the First Law of Nature".

Even in the Sports World, one moment of indiscretion, loss of focus or lack of knowledge can adversely affect your career. This is why you study continuously in all facets of life to be aware of your atmosphere, surroundings & environment to be able to leave & return home safely everyday providing for your family, because sometimes even the hunters become the hunted when they stumble upon the wrong terrain or environment and find themselves no longer at the *"Top of the food Chain!"*.

"When you are a Champion and at the top of your Game or on the Mountaintop, somebody is always painting a target on your back and trying to knock you off."

****Study to show thyself approved!*** *To master your game, you must first become a student of the game. Whatever you want to become, whatever you want to achieve; whatever you want to have, accumulate or acquire they have a book on it. Find a book or books that can help to better your current conditions* *or situations. Read a few Chapters each night towards bettering yourself or your situation. "Study to show thyself approved." Readers are leaders and the reason why is because they are ahead of the game in reference to knowledge & application of that knowledge. The Bible says that the people shall perish for a lack of knowledge. Hosea 4:6. This passage holds true in various facets of life: Spiritual, Social, Physical, Financial, Business and Relationships.*

Special Notes: *There is a difference between reading and studying. Kind of like "entertainment & employment", there is going to be a difference in the level of focus and intensity including the willingness and ability to apply the information received.*

"The only reason men fail is due to broken focus"

****Special Notes:*** *The less you make, the more you need to study! If you don't have at least 50k minimum in your portfolio, savings or 401k, you don't need to watch TV more than 10-12 hours a week. The time used to be entertained can be better utilized to research, enrich or better secure your situation.*

******Special Notes:*** **Have a set of pens {Red, Black, Green; a pad, binder or spiral notebook & highlighters {Yellow, Green & Blue + a voice recorder available when you read this manuscript to take notes and achieve greater results. Take your time to absorb the knowledge that it provides and don't just race or skim through the chapters because the items that you skip could hold the solutions to your challenges. To highly impact your situation, the author suggests reading this book 7-times & no less than 3-times because the first 3-times are most important acquired knowledge} & the next applied knowledge} are for reinforcement & application of the knowledge obtained. Repetition & positive application of knowledge obtained are key ingredients in learning.* ***Some things you read in***

this book will be repeated more than once so that it can manifest into your well being.

Below is a suggested pattern for reading & studying this book to achieve optimal results and a return on your investment of time, energy and resources.

"Study to show thyself approved unto God, a workman who needeth not to be ashamed, rightly dividing the word of truth"-2 Timothy 2:15

Read-React & enjoy, Read & Highlight; Read-Underline & Take Notes; Read-Revaluate & Refresh; Read & Recommend; Read & Re-Purchase/Invest for members of Your Team {so that everybody can be on the same page! Read & WRITE YOUR OWN BOOK {so that you can leave a legacy, make a difference, impact society and position yourself for future endeavors.

COLOR GUIDE

Set of pens:

*{Red *RIGHT NOW!-indicates items or areas that need immediate attention; redirection or application +serious consideration for addition your game plan.*

{Black FUTURE-indicates important concepts & ideas that you feel are important for future growth & development,

{Green VICTORY& FINANCE-indicates any items that can help you to Win, make money, improve your situation or put you in a positive position;

{Blue DISCUSSION-indicates areas that may be topics of discussion and needs revisiting; new information that needs to be researched, shared with others to help their situation or discussed in a round table format.

Highlighters

*{Yellow *PAY ATTENTION/CAUTION/POLISH UP YOUR GAME -indicates areas or items where you need immediate focus, development, attention & improvement.*

{Green GO-indicates any items that motivates you, gets you in gear, inspires you to greatness or that can help you to accomplish the task at hand.

{Light-Blue SPECIAL INTEREST ITEMS-indicates

items or areas that have special meaning, sentimental value or align with your cause or Vision;

{Orange ALERT-indicates items or areas that may be "Time-Sensitive", need "Discretion" or where Decisions have to be made to avoid consequences & Repercussions or where "Life-Lessons" may have been learned {& that you don't repeated.}

"

Chapter 6

MAKE YOUR HEALTH A PRIORITY AND NOT A MINORITY! YOUR HEALTH IS RELATED TO YOUR WEALTH

"I wish above all things that you may prosper and be in good health even as your soul prospers"-3 John 1:2

"You can have all of the $ in the world, but if you don't have health, you don't have Anything!"

"Long life is in her right hand; in her left hand are riches and honor."-Proverbs 3:16

Proper Nutrition & Exercise is Essential not only to good health, but to the image & energy that you exude when you present your program, products & services to others. I remember going to meet an owner of a large internet social media company and while he was having his assistant go over the details of networking with our company with an elaborate power point presentation on his tablet in the hotel lobby of the Hilton, he dropped down and started doing push-ups. That definitely caught my eye. *Many people will go and acquire high dollar material items like houses, boats & automobiles. They will landscape, maintain, wash, & wax it to meticulous standards, fuel it with the choicest premium fuels and oils then go to great detail to make sure these items are insured, secured & garaged to protect their investments but will neglect, misuse ,abuse and under insure their greatest asset which is their body.*

"If you fuel Rolls-Royce dreams with dime-store gas, you will eventually end up on the side of the road waiting for a tow-truck"-Big Ray. www.MillionDollarSideHustle.com

This same thing holds true for your body. Use Wisdom! Proper Maintenance is Essential! If you are going to go out and achieve *"Greatness"* you will have to be in shape not only to go out and get it but also to bring it back home and to maintain it. Learn about the body plus what makes it click and tick. Once you become a master of your body, you can also become a master of your fate and your soul. Your mind, body and soul need to be able to operate in conjunction with one another in addition to your body being able to perform the tasks that mind and soul instructs it to do. To maximize your endurance efforts, many publications recommend that you get in 5-6 days a week of cardio exercise & 3-4 days of weight lifting. One program recommended walking/jogging 1-3 miles daily {morning or evening} and working out in the gym 3-4 times weekly while making sure to work the core muscle groups daily. Included in this program was 100 Push-up, Sit-ups & Deep-knee bends daily + the addition of jumping rope 10-sets of 100 daily. Make sure that you stretch properly and hydrate yourself before exercising. ****Disclaimer: Check with your doctor before you begin any exercise regimen/program or supplemental products! Furthermore, any supplements, exercise regimens, products or services listed in this***

publication are for example purposes only, not endorsed by the author or publisher and to be used at your own discretion.

Chapter 7

KNOW YOUR PERSONNEL

"The most important thing to remember if you want to win a dog fight is to make sure that you bring the right dog"-Yusef L.Chew

As a Coach, leader, mentor, educator, exhorter or manager **it is very important to stay abreast of the moods, mindsets and tendencies of those on your team, inner circle or circumference**. It is your responsibility to **discover what is keeping your personnel from developing to their fullest potential** {on and off of the field of play). **Encourage them to improve** in some area **every day**. **As a leader, it's not always what you know, but more so that of which you teach and how much is absorbed, attained and applied by those whom you lead.**

"How can they know, except that they've been taught,"-Romans 10:15

Special Note: *Create a "Checks & Balance" System so that not only your Team/business is consistent, but everything that's related is double-checked for consistency, quality & clarity. This can help to eliminate problems & reduce challenges before they occur.). Know your personnel and keep in constant contact.* ****Always know what's going***

on in all aspects of your business, financial & personal life + the current trends in your industry. *Regardless of the arena or entity, whether Military; Sports; Corporate America; Personal Relationships or Private Enterprise, you must "Game-Test" all applicants/prospects to show Position worthiness and Battle readiness. Prime example: In the military they have boot-camp; specialized training exercises, mock wars and battlefield simulation operations to gauge the quality of response, aptitude and performance. In sports they have combines, showcases; evaluation- training camps, Off-season Training Activities, scrimmages against each other and against simulated opponents to evaluate talent & potential to operate under stress, duress and game like situations. In the school system they have pop-quizzes & fire drills. In the public sector they have tornado drills/air-raid sirens. In the media they have news-flashes/public-service announcements. In the guise of personal relationships you must "Game-Test" potential mates to make sure that they are not "star-struck" or" fair-weather fans" and in it for the long-haul & not just for short-term benefits or entertainment purposes.*

Chapter 8
DON'T MAKE YOUR PRIORITIES A MINORITY: PREPARE FOR YOUR DESTINY

"***Prior Preparation Prevents Poor Performance***"!

When the Bible makes reference to "*Putting on the Full Armor of GOD, so that you can take your stand against the devil's schemes"-Ephesians 6:11* this is so that you can be equipped to engage in any battle, not just some of them.

"It is better to be prepared for a situation that never comes, than to have a situation come and not be prepared!" -Ron Thompson

Self Discipline is the key to Success!

"If you be willing and obedient, you can eat the good of the land"-Isaiah 1:19

<u>3-THINGS WILL GET YOU BEAT IN THIS GAME:</u> Being Un-disciplined; Un-conditioned and Un-organized!

***<u>Undisciplined:</u>** Discipline is enforced obedience. The first step towards Success is Self-Discipline.

"Without self-discipline success is impossible. Period"-Lou Holtz

"For the Spirit God gave us does not make us timid, but gives us power, love and self-discipline."-2Timothy 1:7

"He dies for lack of discipline, and because of his great folly he is led astray"-Proverbs 5:23

You want the mind to control the body and not the body controlling the mind. You must discipline and strengthen your mind so that it can send the highest quality signals to the body to operate on your behalf in your best interest. **You want your mind strengthened to the point to where it doesn't give in to "*temptations of the flesh*"** and can stay focused on the task at hand to accomplish the goals set forth.

"These Rules may seem wise because they require strong devotion, pious self-denial, and severe bodily discipline. But they provide no help in conquering a person's evil desires or indulgence of the flesh"-Colossians 2:23

The only reason men fail is due to broken focus. You must target that of which you desire the most and pursue it relentlessly. Learn to eliminate Distractions, *Time-Wasters* & *"Fools"* from your schedule. Phase out those who continually distract you from your focus or goal. Identify "*Time-Wasters*" and "*Fools*" then create a system to protect you from them. Deny them access to you and any important information. Anticipate and avoid unnecessary conflicts in addition to never entering into a battle, contest or war where there is no reward. **Always remember that a problem on someone else's part doesn't necessarily constitute an emergency on your behalf**. ***Most problems derive from a lack of adequate preparation for the future, miscommunication or bad habits*.** Keep in mind that Humans are creatures of habit and when put in pressure situations revert back to old habits. Customize your environment to keep yourself focused, motivated & inspired. Create a Daily Success Routine & Habits for Greatness (of which we will go more in depth about in a later chapter).

***Un-conditioned:** *"Your lack of conditioning will make a coward out of you"-Jimmy Johnson.*

You want your body to be in superb shape as not only can you outlast/out-maneuver your opponents or competitors, but as to where your body can perform superbly like a high-performance race car when your brain sends to it high-quality signals. You want your Mind, Will and Emotions conditioned to the point that you will always expect the Best and accept no less than the Best, especially when it comes to Praising GOD, Your Preparation, Performance, Your Productivity & Providing for Your Family. This way, you won't get weary in "*Well-doing*", fold under pressure nor quit in the face of adversity!

The 5-"***P's***" of Conditioning:

***Praise** GOD -Pray & Praise GOD for the victory in advance.

***Prepare /Preparation**

***Perform/Performance**

***Produce/Productivity**

***Provide /Providing/Provision** Provide Results & Provision for your Family.

*Being **Un-organized**: This subject can not only affect your productivity level but your customer/client or fan base and profit margin as well.

"It is better to be prepared for a situation that never happens, than to have a situation happen and not be prepared".*-Ron Thompson*

Always prepare adequately for your destiny! This includes knowing where to be and when to be there; arriving on time or before time with adequate knowledge or prior research of the task at hand. The more organized that you are equates to the more productive you and/ or your business can be in addition to being attractive to potential customers, clients or organizations that could utilize your goods, products or services. You want to organize every facet of your life so that not only everything has a place, but you can be abreast of everything that is going on within your environment and manage accordingly especially in the areas of family, fitness, finance, communication, personnel and security so that you are aware of all activities within to avoid certain pitfalls of life.

8-Ways to Win:

- **Association**
- **Participation**
- **Domination**
- **Acceleration**
- **Location**
- **Destination**
- **Occupation**
- **Game plan/Strategy**

**Get an Organizer, Desk Calendar or create a daily itinerary of things you intend to accomplish each day & check off completed items. Set alarm reminders on your phone calendars & memo sections as a back-up tool.*

*****Special Note: Organize your schedule to eliminate "Time-wasters" & "Distractions". The time wasted with fools can be invested with Winners!***

Chapter 9

STAY CLEAN & KEEP GOOD HYGIENE!

Before you go into Business or Competition, Know the Business that you are entering into and make sure that you are doing things in a Business Like manor in addition to making sure that your Business appears worthwhile & worth doing business with!

"The first step towards making a Million Dollars is a Million Dollar Smile"-Big Ray**.**

Tighten up your "*Grill*" {& not with the kind that the rapper Paul Wall made famous} & Polish Up Your Game in all aspects! Transportation; Occupation, Wardrobe, Appearance, Hobbies, Networks & Associations, Print-Media/Marketing Literature & Business Cards. ***Image is Everything!*** Perception eventually becomes reality. **Everything about you should say that you are Winning before a word even comes out of your mouth**. Upgrade and Invest in yourself! ***("There is no greater physical investment on this earth than in oneself and your offspring").*** Sometimes you have to splurge on a nice outfit or shoes to put your "Best foot forward"! **You have to look & *smell* like a million *{or at least look like you are capable of generating a million}* in order to attract millions.** It's hard to secure million dollar contacts & contracts looking like "*Discount Danny*" with a flea-market suit/swap-meet look or smelling like *dime-store cologne.* You have to look the part. **Every day**

that you leave the house or the office, *its lights, camera, action*! Just as you are constantly evaluating scenarios, situations and surroundings, **someone is always watching you**.

__5-Things That You Should Always Have Control Of:__ A relative of mine once told me when I was younger that "No matter what level you are on or whatever your plight is in life, there are 5-things that you should always have control of:

"Always have your hair combed; Your behind washed, Teeth Brushed, Clothes cleaned & pressed, Shoes shined"!-Theopolis Benefield

Take an extra minute or 2 at least 3-times daily to review your appearance (*as if you were campaigning for office or the Hall of Fame*) and make sure that everything is in order so that when you present your programs, products, goods or services you can put your best foot forward. If your goal is to win the Kentucky Derby, you don't want to go in looking {or smelling) like a donkey; because that's just a behind whipping waiting to happen and you are in it to Win It!

**Get with a graphic arts person and create a business card that is outstanding not necessarily too busy that gives the impression that you are a winner and if put in a fish-bowl of business cards it would get selected. Also look into getting the oversized version {possibly shaped or with rounded* *corners} which makes your card stand out and hard to loose when you give it to someone.*

*Put Some "*Show-Business*" into your Show or Business! : When trying to attract new prospects, customers, clients or patrons, you need to do something to attract a moment of someone's attention. If you see the need to use "*Smoke & Mirrors*" or a few "*props*", then by all means do so because "*if your house catches on fire people will come from miles around to watch it burn down*"! **Do something different to make your business stand out in a crowd or better yet give the consumer something Outstanding to make sure that Your Business Stands Out In Their MIND or is a Memorable Experience!**

Special Note: ***Whatever you promise in your marketing medium or recruiting pitch; make sure that you fully deliver on and don't cut short! Meet, beat or exceed their expectations!***

Chapter 10

IF YOU WANT TO BE GREAT SURROUND YOURSELF WITH GREATNESS

"He who walketh with wise men shall be wise"-Proverbs 13:20

GET THE RIGHT PLAYERS & COACHES ON YOUR TEAM: ALIGN YOURSELF WITH POSITIVE/PRODUCTIVE PEOPLE:

"Success in Life is a Team-Effort"!-Big-Ray.

"Team-Work makes the Dream Work"!-Marshal Fortson

The acronym "T.E.A.M" stands for Together Everybody Achieves More!

"If you want to be Great, surround yourself with Greatness! If you want to be Rich, surround yourself with Riches or Rich People. You usually get what you get around"! -Big-Ray

"The most important thing to remember if you want to win a dog fight is to make sure that you bring the right dog"-Yusef L.Chew

"If you wear a 3-piece suit & nice shoes and work in a barn all day, you will come home smelling like horses & hay"!-Big Ray.

"People make the wrong choices listening to the wrong voices!"-Devin Wyman

With good help being hard to find, always stay in "*Recruit*" mode to **keep quality-effective people on your team**. If you're not networking, you're not working!

"***Sometimes you don't have to be a Rocket Scientist****; sometimes you just need a Rocket!"-Big Ray*

Develop a visual depth chart of all of the different positions you will need assembled on your Team. i.e.; Accountant, Bookkeeper, Financial-Advisor

*{make sure that these 3-positions are held by 3 different individual that are not associated with one another so that you can create a checks & balances system. *Also,* ***Never take financial advice from someone who's income is based on the information that they give you.***},

Attorney {2-3, Marketing Team, Promoters, Webmaster {2-3, Graphic Artists {3-5, Medical Doctor,

*__Hype-Man__ {2-3 minimum}. *This is a very important position on your team! You never know how much you need this person until things get tight or you get behind in the game! You will need one for the fans or in the crowd to rally people around your cause & concessions and another one for the team,* *sales-force or workers! Depending on how big your business/company or entity becomes you will need the 3rd one for yourself when the other 2 are occupied.* ***Leaders need Love, Inspiration, and Motivation & Encouragement too! .*** *Remember, the game whatever line of business that you are in is 90% mental.* ***As a Leader, you need to keep your "creative juices" flowing so that you can keep the business going!*** *Not only do you need to be motivated & inspired to lead, you need a motivated team, sales-staff, congregation or workers, but you need motivated potential prospects & new clientele. Nothing beats a motivated potential prospect that has the willingness and ability to purchase except a paying customer/loyal client . Ideal candidates for this position are: A Pastor/Evangelist, A Coach, A former Athlete or Cheerleader; Used-car Salesmen; Someone who has been successful at Sales/Multi-Level Marketing with good closing techniques; A Radio show host, A popular DJ or someone that has a high level of energy with a lot of enthusiasm that is contagious. The person in this position should have a unique personality, be a great communicator and have a specialized set of skills in that they can graphically illustrate a vision, theme or* ***IDEA*** *in a short amount of time to arouse* ***Interest*** *and have it manifesting within a matter of minutes to create a* ***Desire*** *. Classic illustrations of this concept are: "Someone who could sell water to a whale or ice & igloo's to an Eskimo". In essence you need someone that can preach a good sermon, get the crowd up out of their* *seat, on their feet to cheer* ***Energy/****a change of momentum & put their hands together clapping to give you, your team or cause a standing ovation!* ***Action*** *or motion in the direction of your goal or game-plan*

*Chiropractor {2-3. *Get your spine aligned on a regular basis.* ***It's hard for you to perform at your highest capacity if your body is tight, in pain or not feeling good or Great!*** *Most problems with the body are due to sub-lactations or misalignment of the spine. You want the mind to control the body & not the body controlling the mind. The body is controlled by the brain sending messages through the central nervous system. If the spine is misaligned or a nerve pinched, it could cause certain parts of the body to miss or not receive all of the signals that the brain is sending at the time the signals are sent.*

Barber & Hair-Stylist** {2-3. *Never discount the value of a Great Barber or Hair-Stylist. Not only is "*the quickest way to come up a fresh cut****" as far as image consciousness & self-esteem goes. Now-a-days, your hair-care technician is more than someone that does your hair & keeps you looking good in front of your potential customers & clients. They are an integral part of your business whether you realize it or not? A lot of them have been to college or universities other than Barber & Beauty College. A large portion of them are entrepreneurs & CEO's of their own companies. To stay in business they have had to develop negotiation tactics, conflict* *resolution techniques, marketing, recruitment & communication skills in addition to being able to deal with complex & varied personalities to achieve satisfaction & optimal results. They have to be: an image consultant, fashion expert, a procurement specialist; a confidant, a Spiritual guide; a love-Doctor, cheer-leader, alternative funding source: financial advisor, actor/entertainer hair-shows, marriage counselor, social event guide, Business Referral Partner in addition to being* ***an overall "Solution Specialist".*** *The more diversified their clientele base is, the more valuable they can be to your team. All you have to do is tap into the source and ask questions (& ask for referrals). Chances are that whatever you are looking for to aide you in your business they have connections to and can possibly get you a discounted rate. Not only that, most Successful Barbers & Stylists wants to see you Successful because it would make their business more attractive by having you as a client and mutually beneficial in that it further enhances your ability to subscribe to their services & refer/attract new clients as well. A lot of times back when I was in the hair industry in the off-seasons, I actually made more money from the connections I made in the salon than I made from managing & being a barber-stylist in one. Not only do people from all socio-economic conditions come through Beauty & Barber salons all across America, for those of you caught up in your work, it keeps you in touch with current events & trends.* One time, I actually got hired up out of the salon to go back into coaching football by one of the clients that was an ex-Dallas Cowboy and used to come through & talk *"X's & O's"* in the Barbershop. *That's why it's important to always be on top of your game & have your craft polished because you never know who is observing you?*

*Maid & Janitorial Services {2-3: *They taught us when I was* ***in the Restaurant business*** *that* ***the most important people in the building were the janitor & pot-washer****.*

Personal Trainers {2, Personal Bodyguards/Security on call {3 or more, Personal Drivers/Chauffeur's {2-3, Limo Services on call {2-5, Gym Memberships {1-2,

*Executive Secretary {1-2 *and note, this person needs to be someone that is extremely trustworthy, professional and someone that you don't have an intimate relationship with,*

Dentist, Real-Estate Agent{2-3, Auto-Brokers{3+, Travel agents{2-3, Airline Employees{3+, Hotel Employees{3+, Millionaires {no less than 6, but the more the merrier, Ghost-Writers{2-3, Publicist{2-3, Club Owners {3-5, Restaurant Owner {10+, Professional Athletes {@ least 3 or more in each sport especially Football, Basketball, Baseball, Boxing, Wrestling, Hockey, Moving Company{2-3,

Handyman** {2-3 *Believe it or not,* ***this guy is going to be one of the most important people on your team. *Most people won't appreciate this person until something goes wrong of at which time*

you are going to need a "Solution Specialist". ***The more versatile the person that holds this position is, the better off you are going to be*** *i.e., Paint, clean up, hang drywall/sheet-rock, move furniture, plumbing skills, stand in for security, minor electrical skills, computer repairs skills & more.* ***This person needs to be someone that possess high integrity, extremely trustworthy, professional and someone you can trust with keys to your business to take care of after-hours issues and not give the store/business away nor sell trade secrets to the competition.*** *{Excellent candidates for this position would be middle-aged males with stable backgrounds and family/team oriented like a pastor or little league coach that needs to make some extra $ on the side.*

Attractive Hosts for Special Events {10+ Female & 5-Male, Barbershop & Salon Owners {10-20, Personal Assistants-PA's {2-3,

*Network Marketers{5+/ie;Amway, Primerica, 5-Linx, Avon, Mary Kay, Social Media Zing, Visalis, Kyani, Noni, Pre-Paid Legal, Excel, Herbalife, Stream, Advocare}; *Just like the "Hype-Man" the Network Marketer comes in real handy. A lot of people knock them or avoid them like the "plague" because a lot of people have been conditioned to stay in their disposition & don't want to hear the truth about Corporate America" brain-washing them", being "Modernized-Slavery" or "Trading time for $." I embrace them. A lot of them offer a plan for obtaining wealth in addition to quality products/*

services that enhance the quality of life or save you money over a period of time. On the business side, the ones that have been in business a long time have developed proven $uccess-Systems that if you tap into them you can share some of that $uccess as well! A lot of times as a business owner in the guise of expanding or improving your business you will search out new concepts, ideas or people that you can plug into your business to help it flourish. Beside, a lot of times they have done a lot of the ground work for you and saved you the up-front $. All you have to do is ***observe, take notes & learn!*** *They usually provide a nice venue/place in which to have the events/meetings; They have target-marketed, invited & provided a large group of pre-screened, motivated & enthusiastic business minded people who are open to making extra-$ outside of what they do or need a job.* ***A lot of the people that you will meet at these events will be opinion leaders and people with substantial contacts or a warm-market if you will {This is what they refer to as "Impact-Players", "Game-Changers" or an individual with the ability to change the game and your bank account as a single entity).*** *Next, if the meeting is over 2-3 hours, they sometimes provide a nice lunch/refreshments & samples of their products/services. In addition, they usually fly in a Motivational Speaker, Guest-Speaker or "Hype-Man" that will deliver a Sermon/"Hype-Speech" so compelling & inspiring that has you feeling so great at the end that you will feel like you've just won the*

Super-bowl & want to lay your hard earned $ down at the podium and sign up now! Next they provide advanced training classes and marketing techniques that you could easily adapt and utilize within your own business to help it to grow and prosper. Now if you notice, a lot of these informational meetings also known as "Introduction & Attraction" Sessions will be strategically choreographed/orchestrated as to where they have timed "restroom & water-breaks" where you will meet people you don't know {some who are in the business who want to gauge your level of interest in the business & others who aren't) who want to get your opinion as to what you think about the presentation? This is your opening to Network, ask questions & inquire of the person's background and dispensation. Collect and exchange as many business cards, cell #'s & email addresses as possible during these breaks because at the end of these meeting a lot of the non-enrolled people will cordoned off or pulled over to the side as the person who invited them & their up-line try to persuade, motivate and inspire non-enrollee's to sign up ASAP with a divide & conquer move.

All you have to do is go and visit a few of their major meetings & network to come up. The good thing about most of these meetings is that ***they have prescreened most of the invitees to include people that are "open minded", have their options open for new concepts and idea, plus are "like minded/business minded individuals."*** *Everything or everyone you need to build a team* *usually shows up at these meetings from owners, customers & clients to worker bees. Everybody plays an important part in the ecosystem*

"Everybody you meet can do at least 2-things for you! It's up to you to find out what those 2-things are & fully utilize them to that extent."-Penney St. James

+Special Note: *Don't take this as a sign to join every Multi-level company that comes along, because they aren't for everybody. You don't have to join to benefit from them or the products & services. Besides, you can develop your own Multi-level company just like they did, it just takes effort. Also if they have products or services that can improve your life, are ecologically friendly and/or save you time, energy & resources it's alright to spend a little $ with them on products/services that you were going to acquire anyway. When it comes down to it, people like to spend $ with those that they know or like. In the grand scheme of things, you were going to wash your body, hair, clothes & dishes in addition to use electricity, internet, insurance, cable & cell phone services with or without them. It wouldn't hurt to patronize their business if they are going to patronize yours. You may even run across a Multi-level company that you like and can see yourself profiting from? Remember, everybody has to eat and it's enough out here for everybody to have a smorgasbord or a Buffet!* ***The word for today is***

"Mutually-Beneficial!" *What is it to spend a couple of hundred dollars on some soap-products or otherwise with someone who will turn around and spend Thousands with you?*

*Party Promoters {5-10; *These are usually people who have large followings & databases. As you mature, get older or more prominent in your business you will have less time or desire to hit every party that comes along. For less than a few hundred dollars on the average you can cross-promote/ tap into their databases or onto their print mediums and present your marketing message to the multitudes for less time, energy & effort than it would have taken you to do it yourself. Most promoters won't mind assisting you because not only will they have a new client, but they can take your small seed & multiply it up to times ten making this venture "Mutually Beneficial."*

Special Note:** Before approaching a promoter about cross-promoting make sure that your product, service or marketing message doesn't cause a conflict of interest nor conflict with your standards, morals, values, ethics or religious beliefs? Sometimes it's better to pay extra up front and get a direct promoter or marketing medium to advertise your goods & service than to portray an image contradictory to that intended.

Uniform manufacturers {3+, Energy Drink manufacturers {2-3, Sports Drink Suppliers {2-3,

Sports Shoe Representatives {3+, Screen Printers {3+, Comedians {7+, Professional Singers {7+, Parking Valet companies {2-3, Chefs{3+, Catering companies {3+, BBQ-Cooks{3-5, Event Planners {3, Book Authors{5+, Skin-Care Manufacturers{3+, Pastors{7+, Concert Promoters {5+, Play Writers {3+, DJ's {4+, Electrician{2, Plumber{2, Computer Technician{2-3,

Special Note: ***If you can find a person or individuals that can do 3+ or more of the above as a single entity and still be highly effective, you have found what we like to call an "Impact-Player", Franchise-Player, Superstar or Super-Hero!*** *These are people who can play multiple positions and still achieve optimal Results! If you are going to develop a* ***CHAMPIONSHIP TEAM*** *it pays to have some* ***Team Players with Superstar Qualities!*** *(You don't want too many Superstars, just Team members with Superstar qualities to achieve balance & equilibrium. You do not want egos & attitudes getting in the way of progress or Success!) Remember that* ***everybody on the Team plays an important part.*** *Later on in this book The Acknowledgements Chapter aka "****The Treasure Chapter****" I will introduce you to some of the people on my team that have helped me to become $uccessful and if you need assistance mention that you heard about them from the author or by reading this book and turn some of your challenges into $olutions! {If you talk to them nice & ask for the "Big-Ray $pecial" you'll be surprised at* *what you might get! They may be able to help you to find some $olutions to your challenges at a reduced rate.*

***** Special Note: Do not forget to reward, recognize or give a "Love-offering" periodically to your team-members or associates when you are Victorious or for a job well done. Also, if things ever get tight, these are the people that you will reach out to call on favors. Remember Rich people call in favors, Poor people don't!***

******Special Note: Team up with people that accessorize your limitations and accentuate your weaknesses. Also, make sure that their philosophy harmonizes with your objectives.***

Chapter 11
VISUALIZE ON WINNING THE PRIZE!

"Finally brethren, whatsoever things are true, whatsoever things are honest, whatsoever things are just, whatsoever things are pure, whatsoever things are lovely, whatsoever things are of good report; if there be any virtue, and if there be any praise, think on these things."-Philippians 4:8

"Where there is no vision, the people shall perish..."-Proverbs 29:18

"Commit to the Lord whatever you do and He will establish Your Plans"-Proverbs 16:3

*__In order to win__ or acquire the "***Big-One***" you must first see yourself accomplishing this task. **You must have a mind to Prosper and a Will to Win.**

"Life is not made up of "the haves" and "the have-nots", but more so "the wills" and "the will-not".-Big Ray

The only reason men fail is due to broken focus. You must target that of which you desire the most and pursue it relentlessly.

Don't let the opinions of the average man sway you. Dream and he thinks you're crazy. Succeed and he thinks you're lucky. Acquire wealth and he thinks you're greedy. Pay no attention, and they simply don't understand. Complaining people focus on the wrong things. Happiness is not an accident, nor is it something you wish for. Happiness is something you design!

Anticipate and avoid unnecessary conflicts in addition to never entering into a battle, contest or war where there is no reward.

*CREATE A VISION BOARD & UPDATE IT ON A REGULAR BASIS

"Write The Things Which Thou Hast Seen, And The Things Which are, And The Things Which Shall Be Hereafter."-Revelation 1:19

"You cannot solve a problem from the same consciousness that caused it. You must see the world anew."-Albert Einstein

Create a Vision Board to keep your Goals, Dreams and Aspirations alive & motivated. In the Bible there are parables that make reference to *"Without a vision the people shall perish" and "Write the vision down and make it plain to see..."* Habakkuk 3: Your vision board should illustrate & encompass parts of your game plan, mid-range and long-term goals in addition to pictures or illustrations of things that you want to acquire and where you want to be in the future. As you develop your Team, organization or business entity, your marketing mix and promotional mediums will encompass some of these things on your vision board to stimulate new growth in business. In a Marketing curriculum we were taught that "visual is 93% of your presentation."

"Proper Presentation along with Prior Preparation Prevents Poor Performance"

Just as some people utilize video/ film sessions or issue out *"flow-charts" or "Playbooks"* to their Teams or Organization to give them a *"Picture"* or a visual perception of how things should go to make things transition smoother, encompassing this concept along with your Coaching techniques, Vision or *"Vision board"* can add the same effect.

"A picture is worth a Thousand words!"

Chapter 12
ALWAYS TAKE CARE OF HOME & LOOK OUT FOR THE HOME TEAM

Always take care of Home!** *Never get so caught up in the Business or outside world as to where you neglect or forget the real reason "Why***" you are doing this in the first place.* **Home is where the heart is.** *If home isn't taken care of in all aspects, either you are doing too much or not enough!*

In addition to taking care of home, make sure that you have adequate security mechanisms (including hidden cameras/microphones) in your home, business & office. *They now have the systems where you can check your home or business from the other side of the world via cell phone, laptop or computer. Remember the root of Security is: "Secure-it." A word to the wise should be sufficient! Also as you ascend the ladder of affluence make sure that you have an "armor bearer" on the team/speed-dial or someone that can double in that capacity until you develop a need to acquire personal or executive security. Ex-College football players serve well in this capacity. Not only are they educated and have the physique, but a team concept as well.*

Chapter 13
DON'T LET THE GAME PLAY YOU.

Anticipate and avoid unnecessary conflicts in addition to never entering into a battle, contest or war where there is no reward.

Learn the Business side of the game and the typical life-cycle span of your particular industry so that you can approach it in a proper perspective and exit or elevate gracefully when it's time to move around. A lot of people disillusion themselves with false hopes & aspirations. Always have a "Plan-B" as well as an "Exit-Strategy" at hand. When you set your goals for the future, make sure that they are realistic and consider the different stages of the Life Cycle and adjust your plans according to your ability to perform, produce or motivate others to do the same. Remember that Success is not always about prestige or material items, but more so the progressive attainment & achievement of ones goals in addition to being able to provide for your family. The Championship Rings, Trophies & Checks are nice, but Life is about the Journey, the People that you meet along the way and the Legacy that you leave behind.

Chapter 14

LEAVE A LEGACY

Write a Book on whatever you're Good at and leave a legacy. *Don't let your history be a mystery. Remember "the game is to be sold, not to be told and when you tell it, make sure that you sell it & make sure that you (and everybody associated) gets their cut/fair-share!"*

Not only does becoming an author put you in a select segment of society, it legitimizes your projects in addition to positioning you as an expert at what you do. ***Your book can go places that you can't go*** in addition to opening doors that were previously inaccessible and it's something that can stand the test of time. Write a Book. **Every Successful person should have at least 1-book credit to their name!** *If you're famous or successful, someone is going to write a book or a short story on you anyway so why wait until you die to multiply or enjoy the cash flow* You can't take it with you and you don't see armored cars following hearses or funeral processions. Whatever you have a passion for, write a book on it. Write a book on your persuasions, talents or gifts.

*"**A man's gift makes room for him and brings him before great men**"-Proverbs 18:16*

Another way to leave a legacy is to be a difference maker and a problem solver. Most people will be remembered for the problems that they have solved or the ones that they've created. Let every life that you touch or person that you influence become better as a result of coming into contact with you. Leave every situation that you enter or encounter better than when you found it.

***Special Note:* Remember that Success is not always about prestige or material items, but more so the progressive attainment & achievement of ones goals in addition to being able to provide for your family. The Championship Rings, Trophies & Checks are nice, but Life is about the Journey, the People that you meet along the way and the Legacy that you leave behind.**

Chapter 15

MAKE EVERYDAY PAYDAY WHETHER YOU'RE WORKING OR NOT.

*Make Everyday Payday whether you're working or not. *Find out what Residual Income is. Also living paycheck-to-paycheck is alright as long as its daily paychecks!*

Learn how to get on the other side of money and set yourself up for $uccess! A lot of people wake up and go to work for their money, while others go to sleep at night while their money works for them. It's a difference and a Big-Difference! Many people wake up in the morning, get dressed then travel on the mazes or highways & by-ways of America to chase "*Cheese/checks*" in the proverbial "*rat-race*" sometimes referred to as "*Corporate America*" or trading time for money. Other people wake up, workout, have a good breakfast and then call the bank or their financial services provider to count their money then set a game-plan in reference as how to enjoy life & the day more abundantly. {*Not saying that they don't have to work, but* ***life is a whole lot easier when you have a few irons in the fire working for you and you don't have to operate under stress, duress or be pressed for time or your dime.*** *Instead of chasing carrots, you can grow a carrot patch. Instead of chasing "checks & cheese" You can check write at your delight and* *have the "checks & cheese" chase you the way it's supposed to be if you're on top of your game. Prime example was Shaq in his prime and even after he resigned. He was always on top of his game and his name was in the game which caused teams, people, products and services to constantly seek his attention/services for hire/desire or money to wire! Also, over a million pairs of shoes with his name on them have been sold over a decade after he has retired from the NBA.}*

Some people do what they want to do and others do what they have to do. This is the difference between Successful & Stressful!

Chapter 16

USE IT BEFORE YOU LOOSE IT!

Everybody has been issued a certain measure of gifts or talents in addition to having a life cycle with an Expiration date {like milk. **A lot of times you will hear people near the end of their career state that *"if I knew what I know now back then, I would have did things different and been much further ahead in life"*.**

A prime example of this are **Pro-Athletes, Actors & Dancers** of which have an average career span of 3-5 years. **Most of them are coached or conditioned to believe that they are "*invincible & unbeatable*" in their respective crafts and think that they can compete for a lengthy career**. While some Great ones have surpassed the 5-year mark, a lot have never made it to the 2 ½ -3 years necessary to acquire a pension. You will hear a lot of people say that *"The NFL stands for Not For Long!"* The major irony of this situation is that while a lot of them are at the pinnacle of their careers , they fail to begin with the end in mind by having an exit strategy or a "***Plan-B***" back-up plan just in case the dream ends prematurely or a nightmare injury or situation erupts. **The** other **sad part of the situation is that a lot of them blow huge amounts of cash** like it's *"Monopoly-Money"* **on non-functional jewelry, self-depreciating material items, cars & overpriced wardrobe items instead of investing adequately for the**

future so that their money can work for them instead of them having to work for money {or someone else} after their illustrious career is over.

One of the things that people seem to take for granted, don't use wisely or don't take account for is "***Time.***" Just as there are various seasons and levels in the "*Life-cycle*", there is a time and a place for everything. "***Time***" **is a valuable commodity, which once loss, can never be regained or redeemed.** I have told a lot of my former players on several occasions that "*Time, honeys & money wait on no man, and neither do scholarships or contracts.*" The worst thing to see is a player or athlete past his "*prime*" still trying to live the dream like he was fresh out of college when in actuality, he is "*washed up like detergent*", stuck in a time warp and has no plan or provision to make a smooth transition into the future. Each level in the "*Life-cycle*" has various experiences and lessons for us to encompass which often times helps us to develop, mature, metamorphosis in addition to preparing us for future endeavors & experiences. A prime example of this is one of my former players who at the age of 40 were a "*free* agent" & still trying to play professional football. On the outside, he looked like the perfect specimen or as we say "*passed the eyeball test*" {which meant that he looked the part} and appeared to be in better shape than a lot of the "*youngsters*" due to a consistent regimen of working out in the weight room. What he didn't take into account for was that with the game of Football being a "*Collision Sport*" and barbaric in nature, the Human body wasn't designed to take "*pain & punishment*" more than a few seasons in the Life cycle nor the rigors of running around on artificial turf past a certain age. Even though the player's mindset and approach were very energetic & enthusiastic, his mind, body and soul weren't on the same page and consequently, he experienced a serious career ending knee injury which took major surgery and a few months of rehab in order for him to walk again. Fortunately for him, he had an entrepreneurial venture in place and the right people on his personal team to sustain him during the setback. Moral of the story is as we've said in other chapters, "*Know what game you're playing before you begin" and "Adapt & Adjust your game to fit the terrain." It's nothing wrong when chasing the dream, but if it hasn't developed or manifested {or looks close to reaching the goal} by the deadline, it's time to move around.* Develop insight & awareness so as to notice and discern the changing of the seasons and operate appropriately in each.

***<u>*Special Note:</u>* Learn the Business side of the game and the typical life-cycle span of your particular industry so that you can approach it in a proper perspective and exit or elevate gracefully when it's time to move around. A lot of people disillusion themselves with false hopes & aspirations. Always have a "Plan-B"**

as well as an "Exit-Strategy" at hand. When you set your goals for the future, make sure that they are realistic and consider the different stages of the Life Cycle and adjust your plans according to your ability to perform, produce or motivate others to do the same. Remember that Success is not always about prestige or material items, but more so the progressive attainment & achievement of ones goals in addition to being able to provide for your family. The Championship Rings, Trophies & Checks are nice, but Life is about the Journey, the People that you meet along the way and the Legacy that you leave behind.

Chapter 17
TURN HATERS INTO PARTICIPATORS

"They hate us because they ain't us."

The acronym "***HATERS"*** *stands for* "***Having Anger Towards*** *those* ***Enjoying Real Successes."***

Everybody plays an important part in the Ecosystem. *{Utilize haters to their fullest extent while keeping things in their proper perspective to accomplish your goals.* Some of the ***main reasons that people hate are that they Jealous or Envious, want to be you, be like you or acquire the things that you have.*** Other reasons may be that "*haters"* are "***Miserable***" *and* tired of losing while you're "*Winning*" or tired of losing to you!

In order to turn haters {or anyone else for that matter) into participators, you must first develop your ability to put yourself into other people's shoes, rationalize on their way of thinking and point of view or proverbially *"trade minds with them".* Ask yourself," *If I were a typical hater, what is it that I wouldn't like about myself and what is it that I have, that they want. What is it subconsciously that possibly could have them envying me or wanting to be like me?"* Looking at things from their background, dispensation, viewpoint or perspective;

how would you perceive or react to my approach & demeanor? Once you know how their mind flows or thought patterns travel, you can utilize this knowledge to *transform some of them* into a functional ally or an additional fan in the fan base. As for those loyal *"die-hard"* fans of the opposition that you are unable to transition to your team or way of thinking, don't worry about it. Somebody has to play the opposition/ competitor role and remember that everybody plays an important part in the ecosystem. {Just make sure that every time that they oppose you that they come up on the losing end!

Chapter 18
TREAT LOYALTY LIKE ROYALTY

"Good Help is Hard to Find!"-Dorothy Hardy

Treat Loyalty Like Royalty!* *As my mother always said "Good Help is Hard to Find:"! When you find someone that's loyal to you or your team and not just liking you for your paper or the things that you can do, take the time as often as possible to reward and let that person know that they are very much appreciated.* ***You will definitely find out who your true friends are when you lose the limelight or things get tight!* *It's always good to have Good People on Your Team! You never know when you are going to need them to make a play or call on them for a favor?*

Design your game plan so that it's rewarding for those on your team to be in your presence in addition to those on your support staff and others who subscribe to your theories, products, goods and services. Be aware of the things that spark delight in those that are loyal to you {especially those in your family, staff, team and fans}, then do what's in your power to provide its consistent presence in their life (*as long as it's legal, moral & ethical or doesn't cause them to falter.*

Invest in things that will keep those loyal to you motivated and inspired. You will be surprised as to what something as small as a t-shirt, a hat; a pen; gift card/ gas card or a dozen of Roses can do to lift a person's spirits. You will find that as you work hard to achieve your highest potential, it will be more meaningful when you share with those that are loyal to you and your program. Besides, you never know when the tables will be turned and you could be in a position of needing assistance. I have seen several instances of where former players have hired their former coaches (& vice versa) to come and work or coach for them in some capacity because of the loyalty and respect developed from prior relationships.

Chapter 19

STRAP UP BEFORE YOU TAP UP!

"Life is a Contact Sport. Protect yourself at all times in all facets of life."

"SELF-PRESERVATION IS THE FIRST LAW OF NATURE!"

In life when you are about to enter into competitive, tense or even hostile situations or environments, make sure that you are adequately prepared and have all protective measures, garments & equipment in place. In the Spiritual realm, the Bible states *"to put on the full amour of God."* When operating motor vehicles or motorcycles make sure that you do a visual inspection of the vehicle and make sure that they are well maintained and have good tires in addition to taking proper safety measures such as seat-belts or helmets. In or on the field of Athletics *especially "Contact or Collision" Sports* it is highly recommended to bring at least 3-mouthpieces and insert one in addition to making sure that all pads, shoes; helmets, cups & supporters if applicable are in place and strapped up securely to prevent injuries because one slip up can cost you your career. In Law Enforcement & the Military, never get so comfortable or complacent with your environment that you forget or neglect to wear and take adequate protection methods ***like that vest, helmet, tools***

& accessories to increase the odds of returning home in one piece.

In interpersonal relationships ***especially if you're not married*** most definitely make sure that you take extra measures to ***"Protect Yourself at All Times"!*** *{Make sure that consent forms or waivers are signed, Use personal protection & check ID's.* The Life you save may be your own & **one *"Slip-Up"*** could result in wage garnishments +you paying a 20 year mortgage in support *or worse, a 20-year bid*! On your material possessions such as cars, boats, planes & high-dollar electronic items or even tires, make sure that they are adequately insured and have adequate warranties in place. This measure will reduce future headaches and expenses.

Chapter 20

DON'T CHASE EM', REPLACE THEM! DON'T SWEAT EM', LET EM'!

*"**If your Presence can't add Value or Joy to my Life, Your Absence will make no difference!**"-Big Ray*

One of my mottos in life is that "***I don't chase Players, Honeys or Money***"*!* I don't chase "***Players***" because there is a new one born every day. I don't chase "***Honeys***" because they are in surplus, *"A dime a dozen & 30-for a Quarter".*

"They make new Honeys just like they make New Money, Everyday!"-Big Ray

"I never get jealous when I see my ex with someone else, because my parents always taught me to give my used toys to the less fortunate."-A J. Suttles

It's a "***Honey***" around every corner and they have them ***on special everyday at Wal-Mart***. If you don't believe me go to Wal-Mart during Happy Hour *{3:30pm-7:30pm then go to the deli or produce section and smile. If you are looking for one that's more affluent,* go next door to Sam's Club or Costco's.

"The time you use to sweat a honey could be used to make some money."-Big Ray
www.MillionDollarSideHustle.com

"Chasing skirts might make your money hurt, but making money ain't never hurt a skirt!"-Big Ray

Sometimes you have to disconnect yourself from people or things emotionally in certain situations so that you can complete the task/job at hand.

I don't chase "***Money***" because it is a medium of exchange and not worth the paper it's printed on and its purpose is to be a servant and work for you on assignment & not the other way around. Besides they have a Mint that prints $'s by the Bank-Roll 6-7 days a week. It's plenty more where it came from contrary to popular belief of a shortage created by the media. If anyone is going hungry or experiencing a shortage, this stems from a lack of adequate preparation for the future.

*<u>*Special Note:</u>* **Understand that you always must be in control of your destiny and not let destiny control you.** Never jump for $ or appear desperate. *Never let a prospect or project manipulate or pressure you into any situation.* No matter how much money you are offered or need, never let anyone use money to control you. ***Money is a tool that you can use and an inanimate object, but it doesn't come with instructions! It is supposed to serve and work for you instead of you serving and working for it***. You are supposed to give $ assignments and tasks to

complete. Money is a resource and a reward for solving problems for others, not a source. Know where your true source is and where your blessings & power come from.

No man can serve both GOD and mammon.

"...Choose you this day whom you shall serve, as for me and my house, We Will Serve The Lord!" –Joshua 24:15

Chapter 21
IF YOU WANT DIFFERENT RESULTS, DO SOMETHING DIFFERENT!

One of the **definitions of Insanity is *"Doing the same thing over & over but yet expecting a different result!"***

{Don't get this confused with consistency because some things take time and is not always an overnight sensation. If you're working on a project and you are experiencing a *"growth & development"* spurt or seeing progress then stick to the script. But if the script isn't working change the ending. Change is inevitable. Sometimes it is better to embrace change rather than to have it instituted upon you. ***If you get up and go to work every day and it's not working, ask yourself why?*** A lot of people will beat a proverbial *"dead horse"* on a *"dead-end job"* hoping that things will eventually get better but end up putting themselves deeper into a hole when all that they had to do was *change their location or occupation to improve their situation*. What a lot of people don't understand is that "***sometimes all it takes to change your year is to change your atmosphere***." A prime example of this is when I was working in corporate America for a major corporation {company-A} making what I thought was decent $ at the time when a former coworker from a previous company {company-D} called me and recruited me to come to {company-C} where he was now working. He went into great detail as to the immediate as well as the long term benefits of changing locations & occupation from {company-A} which resulted in an immediate increase of 12k + signing bonus and an additional approximate 50k+ increase over the year after you ad in bonuses, incentives and unlimited overtime {+*"flex time"* which meant that I could come and go as I pleased as long as I was productive. ***One of the main reasons that you go to work is to make $*** and more $ gives you more options. That additional increase parlayed & *"flipped"* over 3-years without a significant increase in living expenses has allowed the author to go into early retirement, travel and enjoy Life to the fullest extent. As they tell you in Real Estate as well as Business, ***"Location, Location, Location!"*** The same effort that it takes to make a *minimum* in one market can be utilized to make millions in another one. **Check out the upcoming book *"The 7-Figure/Million Dollar - Side Hustle"*** www.MillionDollarSideHustle.com and change your life as well because you can't ball forever, but you can incorporate some of these principles and **enjoy a *"Winning Lifestyle*' for a Lifetime.**

Chapter 22

KEEP YOUR NAME IN THE GAME & CAMPAIGN LIKE YOU'RE TRYING TO MAKE THE HALL OF FAME!

Protect Your Name! It is going to outlast you!

"When people hear your name, they need to know who you are and that you're Good at what you do!"-Big Ray www.BigRayInternational.com

"A good name and reputation is more powerful than money" (Proverbs 22:1)

Campaign Like You're Trying to Make the Hall of Fame!

Always be in "Recruit" mode. "When growth stops, decays starts!"

"If you put out 1000+ flyers a week, you will never go hungry"-Joan Louis.

A name is nothing unless people can associate it with something *Extraordinary; Some Unique Talent or Knowledge*.

"It's not always who you know or what you know, but more so who knows you & to whom you are connected to that matters!"

Ask yourself, *"Are you content with being a local celebrity or are you trying to be World Famous at what you do?"* If you've had some semblance of success and or you have a "*passion for the game that you're in"*, when you're playing or working days are over doesn't necessarily mean that you have to leave the industry. Elevate you game and operate in an alternative capacity. Some players move up into Coaching, Administration or some type of ownership capacity after their playing career is done. Others may choose to become mentors, trainers, consultants or agents when their illustrious careers have ended while some go into sports marketing, broadcasting or operations. There are so many facets to the game to be encompassed of which the possibilities are endless. Whether you are in the game or retired from the game, don't just be an ambassador to the game when you can become President. It doesn't matter whether you're active, retired or newly hired, when people hear your name, they need to know who you are and that *"You're Good at what you do!"*

Chapter 23
WHEN COMPETITION BEGINS, FRIENDSHIP ENDS.

"Many people take competition for granted, but competition breeds Champions!"-Norman Whitfield

I've always told people when I was Coaching Football,

"This is Not a Nice Game!"

What that means is that *somebody is going to "Win" and somebody is going to "Learn"*. Somebody is going to get their feelings hurt, egos crushed and dreams demolished. When you compete, it's not about being liked or loved, but being respected. I remember when I used to own a Barber Salon that an *"associate"* who had a similar business in the vicinity used to tell me

"Ain't no friends in Business!"

Which goes to say or imply is *that whenever someone opposes you, whether in Business, Life or on the court or playing field, one thing that they need to know is that you're going to try to take their head off so to speak or do your best to crush them in head to head competition."* Prime example of this is when I was in the *"Hair-Game."* I issued out service & styles so superior to that of my competitors that it was not only visually but physically evident as well. The competition and the customer base knew who I was and what I had to offer from being on top of my game. This doesn't mean don't have some class about yourself.

"Let all things be done decently and in order"-1 Corinthians 14:40

If you're in a game and up by 40-50 points in the 4th Quarter by all means put the reserves in and let them get some experience and development ***unless the opposition is a fierce rival or said /did something derogatory in the past in which case you have to teach them a lesson and run the score up*** **like a *"Las Vegas slot-machine"*& rub their nose in it like *a puppy dog that has pooped in the wrong place* to teach a lesson.**

A real life example of this is when I was coaching Arena Football and we were ranked near the top of our division after knocking off the two-time defending League Champions in regular season. It just so happened that our next opponent who we had to play back to back was winless, had less talent and was now being coached by our previous Head Coach who was recently acquired. Prior to the first game after we arrived at their place, the former Head Coach of our team came and greeted all of our players hugging & loving on them like they were his son's and we were all related *a term our current Head Coach referred to as "brother-in-lawing"*. End result is that we played the game like we were competing against a close relative, confidant, friend or neighbor instead of against an opponent that was trying to take us out of business, relieve us of our livelihoods and get their first win of the year. We succumbed to their level of play & made their team owner look like a Genius and our former Head Coach look like a savior. That night we didn't possess that "***Killer-Instinct***" or aggressive action needed to compete on this level and lost the game to an inferior opponent by 4 points. The next week our current Head Coach called practice on one of our team's off days to give them *"the business"* for a lack-luster performance and 8-players decided not to show up. After practice, we called in some *"free-agents"* that were hungry and wanted to work to replace those who didn't want to work. At the next practice session the current players noticed all of the new faces from new places and got the message:

"***Produce or get reduced!"-Big Ray*** ***www.Chosen1Sports.com***

"Motivation is simple. ***Eliminate those who aren't motivated!****"-Lou Holtz*

During the upcoming week the current Head Coach had the team work extra hard and attend long film sessions. He stressed the importance of focus, execution and completing assignments in the proper fashion from start to finish in addition to reiterating the reason why we are here. Prior to the next game at home, our current Head Coach let it be known that we were preparing for a Battle and that **the guy that we used to know and love in the opposite**

color uniform was not here to be our friend or *buddy* during the next 60-minutes but more so to steal *or kill* our dreams & aspirations, put us out of business and have us standing in the *"soup-line!"* Word was conveyed to our former Head Coach *by yours truly* that our new Head Coach respectfully requested that he refrain from entering our locker room and to postpone from fraternizing or fellowshipping with the players until after the game ends to maintain a mental balance needed for competition. The former Head Coach was *a little salty*, but he understood, especially after we *"**tattooed their behinds with a 53-point**"* margin of victory in one of our highest scoring contests of the year {84-points) to win the game. After the game, the former coach was non-existent and disappeared quickly into the night to face reality on that long road trip home that ***"Self-Preservation is a #1 Priority and the 1st Law of Nature!"*** These **men had families to feed and bills to pay & being nice in competition wasn't going to help them to keep their jobs nor the lights on!**

"The game is 90% mental! The other 10% is a Dog-fight!"

"When you find yourself in a Dog-Fight, make sure that you're the Dog that Bites!"*-Big Ray*

"I need you in attack-mode and not snack-mode! We're trying to feed a family & not just give them a piece of candy!"-Big Ray

"The most important thing to remember if you want to win a dog fight is to make sure that you bring the right dog"-Yusef L.Chew

Anticipate and avoid unnecessary conflicts in addition to never entering into a battle, contest or war where there is no reward.

Chapter 24
DRESS FOR SUCCESS: Look The Part and Play The Part Well.

Before you go into Business or Competition, Know the Business that you are entering into and make sure that you are doing things in a Business Like manor in addition to making sure that You and Your Business appears worthwhile and worth doing business with!

***"The first step towards making a Million Dollars is a Million Dollar Smile"-Big Ray*.**

Tighten up your "Grill" {and not with the kind that the rapper Paul Wall made famous} & Polish Up Your Game in all aspects: Transportation, Occupation, Wardrobe, Appearance, Hobbies, Networks & Associations, Print-Media/Marketing Literature & Business Cards. *Image is Everything*! Perception eventually becomes reality. Everything about you should say that you are "*Winning"* before a word even comes out of your mouth. Upgrade and Invest in yourself! *"There is no greater physical investment on this earth than in oneself and your offspring."* Sometimes you have to splurge on a nice outfit or shoes to put your "Best foot forward!" You have to look like a million *{or at least look like you are capable of generating a million}* in order to attract millions. It's hard to secure million dollar contacts & contracts looking like *"Discount Danny"* with a flea-market suit/swap-meet look. You have to look the part. Every day that you leave the house or the office, its lights, camera, action! Just as you are constantly evaluating scenarios, situations and surroundings, someone is always watching you.

5-Things That You Should Always Have Control Of: A relative of mine once told me when I was younger that "No matter what level you are on or whatever you plight is in life, there are 5-things that you should always have control of: ***"Always have your hair combed, Your behind washed, Teeth Brushed, Clothes cleaned & pressed, Shoes shined!"-Theopolis Benefield***

Take an extra minute or 2 at least 3-times daily to review your appearance (*as if you were campaigning for office*) and make sure that everything is in order so that when you present your products, goods or services you can put your best foot forward. **If your goal is to win the Kentucky Derby, you don't want to go in looking like a donkey; because that's just a behind whipping waiting to happen and you are in it to Win It!**

**Get with a graphic arts person and create a business card that is outstanding not necessarily too busy that gives the impression that you are a winner and if put in a fish-bowl of business cards it would get selected. Also look into getting the* *oversized version which makes your card hard to lose when you give it to someone.*

*Put Some *Show-Business* into your Show or Business! When trying to attract new Recruits, Coaches, customers, clients or patrons, you need to do something to attract a moment of someone's attention. If you see the need to use *"Smoke & Mirrors"* or a few *"props"*, then by all means do so because "if your house catches on fire people will come from miles around to watch it burn down"! Do something different *to* ***make your business/program stand out in a crowd*** *or better yet* ***give the consumer something Outstanding*** *to* ***make sure that Your Business/Program Stands out in Their MIND or is a Memorable Experience!*** This is what you call that **"*Wow*" factor** which means that you want your audience so astonished that they go back and tell family & friends about their experience. In one corporate setting, we were instructed to ***"Woo, Wow & Win"*** **the client or customer's patronage or business by exceeding above their expectations.**

Special Note: *Whatever you promise in your marketing medium, make sure that you fully deliver on and don't cut short! Meet, beat or exceed their expectations!*

****Special Note:** In order to be "Big-Time", **sometimes you have to carry Big-Time!** In the guise of appearance, that suit, that watch, those shoes, that car, they need to tell a story. That cuts down on a lot of talking. Don't play yourself cheap. When people check out your suit, your shoes, your watch, or mode of transportation it needs to say "Quality!" Your appearance needs to say "VIP", not stand in a line for/or to pay a fee. Look like you're making moves and not like moves are making you.*

Chapter 25

ALWAYS PUT YOURSELF IN POSITION FOR RECOGNITION.

This chapter is self-explanatory, but we will expound upon it anyway to give you further insight. The era that I came up in when I was younger required us to be competitive, especially in the arenas of sports and employment. Long before the days of show up, pay and play (the now generation of sports) or play a get paid a person actually had to prepare for their destiny, tryout for the team and perform well ndenough to get recognized /chosen for the team. *Nepotism in those days meant that you were one of the better players or workers on the team due to the fact that whoever or whomever it was that was responsible for you being there stayed on your behind or in it as a constant reminder so as not to embarrass them or make them look bad for bringing you on board.* Not only did you have to earn your way on the team, but playing time also had to be earned as well. A bad day or a lacksidasical week of practice often resulted in a significant reduction of playing time and /or not dressing for the game. Sometimes you could even get cut in a middle of a season if you weren't performing adequately. This held true from the lower levels like "*Pee-Wee*" & Church League all the way up to the PROS. Even in the job arena most companies hired through a temporary service as a try-out of sorts to assess /evaluate whether you could carry your weight or load. A bad or an off day at work often resulted in a reduction of work hours the next day from 8 to 4 hours or worse yet that call from the temporary service the next morning letting you know that your services were no long required or needed for that assignment. As a player, manager, coach, coordinator, teacher, captain, team-leader or member of a team/organization it is imperative that you always put your best foot forward and/or your best effort forth in any endeavor that you participate in because someone is always watching and evaluating. **When you leave out of your house every day, you are under a microscope!**

"Its Lights, Camera, Action & Showtime!"

Even if you're not the best candidate for a position, look like it. Always look your best perform your best and practice being the Best you can be and before you know it, it will manifest and come to fruition. **Consistency is the key**. Even the Great Martin Luther King said ***"Longevity has its place".*** Even in the guise of relationships you have to put yourself in position to get recognition or pose to get chose by the person whose attention you are seeking. Think about it? Look at your current relationship or social situation. What is it about that person that attracted you to them? Whether it was appearance, attributes, demeanor, productivity, intellect or attitude it was something that made them catch your eye.

****Always Put Yourself in Position for Recognition!***

"It's better to make the News that to be the News!"- Big Ray

When opportunities present themselves to establish your good name, integrity & reputation, seize the moment. A good name and reputation is more powerful than money. (Proverbs 22:1) Basically what we are saying is to provide things honest in the sight of all men and always be productive. This is not a statement to go out & toot your own horn (Proverbs 27:2) but more so to give people value for their money and never try to beat someone out of their money. Your gifts & talents will make a way before great men.

Chapter 26

PLANT *"Jack & The Beanstalk"* SEEDS OF FAITH.

"I pray that you may be active in sharing your faith, so that you will have a full understanding of every good thing we have in Christ" Philemon 1:6

*In the *fable* about *"Jack & The Beanstalk"* it describes and details about a young man who comes across some *magical beans*/seeds that have enormous growing powers that when once planted in soil only needs a drop of water & some sunlight to metamorphosis with fantastic growth & height proportions. To an *average* ***consumer*** you **might** see or **get caught up in the aura, outcome and results of the magical beans/seeds** that you *fail to see the process needed to produce that outcome*. A ***Producer*** on the other hand will notice the process & team work that took place to achieve the outcome or results. **To a *Producer* the seed was viewed as only 1 part of a 4-part equation and required a 5th element to develop. In order to grow, the *seed* needs *soil, water* & *sunlight*. The 5th and most important element is *the person planting the seed in a fertile growth environment where its powers flourish and ripen* to achieve ultimate results.**

In Life, if you change the way you look at situations or circumstances from different angles you will sometimes discover opportunities that you may have previously overlooked? This is why in the Sports World we roll back the film so that we can find our mistakes and correct them.

Another example of this is when I was in the Restaurant industry and we went through various levels of training for Restaurant Management/Ownership including Production Management. To an average consumer you might walk into a restaurant and count the customers to develop a theory of how much the restaurant is pulling in. To a Producer, he might observe the number of employees present and multiplies it by the going work rate and then again by the number of times the armored car comes by to pick up $ to get a better picture of how much the unit is bringing in to access if it's a worthwhile venture.

Special Note: *There are Special Gifts that GOD has placed within all of us that will generate everything that we need to be Successful, but we must commit to cultivate and grow these seeded gifts from within. Champions are people who have discovered their God-given talents & gifts and committed to taking the time to develop them to receive the benefits associated.*

Chapter 27

BUSINESS & PERSONAL DON'T MIX unless you're married or closely related.

Remember that Business & Personal Business don't always mix! Unless you're married or closely related or If it's not a family owned business,* ***keep your business and your family totally separated {especially the financial purse-strings**) until it's time to bring an offspring up and teach them how to take over the business.* ***Only those closest to you can hurt you*** *and it's often harder to retaliate or take legal action against a relative because you might be the same one having to bail them out or pay their hospital bill or legal fees!*

*****Special Note:**** **In a lot of Businesses {especially Restaurant & Retail}, 18-20% of profits are lost due to theft or Employee pilferage. Do not put people in a position of where they will feel comfortable taking from you because they think they're exempt from "consequences & repercussions." Prevention is better than the cure.***

Chapter 28

LEARN TO ELIMINATE TIME WASTERS &GET RID OF THOSE THAT DON'T RESPECT YOUR TIME OR YOUR DIME.

"Time is a Valuable Commodity when once lost, can never be regained nor redeemed! Use it wisely!"-*Big Ray*

*"**Don't give quality time to unqualified people**"-Charisse L.Brown*

The only reason men fail is due to broken focus. You must target that of which you desire the most and pursue it relentlessly. Learn to **eliminate Distractions, *Time-Wasters* & *"Fools"*** from your schedule. Phase out those who continually distract you from your focus or goal. Identify "*Time-Wasters*" and "*Fools*" then create a system to protect you from them. Deny them access to you and any important information. Anticipate and avoid unnecessary conflicts in addition to never entering into a battle, contest or war where there is no reward. Always remember that a problem on someone else's part doesn't necessarily constitute an emergency on your behalf. Most problems derive from a lack of adequate preparation for the future or bad habits. Keep in mind that Humans are creatures of habit and when put in pressure situations revert back to old habits. Customize your environment to keep yourself focused, motivated & inspired. Create a Daily

Success Routine and Habits for Greatness (of which we will go more in depth about in another chapter.

****Special Note**:* *"Whenever you see a fool, put plenty of space between you and them because they are an accident waiting to happen. Whenever you meet a fool, don't argue or talk with them because they will have you doing something "Foolish". Leave them where you found them & don't travel with them nor have them as companions."-Big Ray*

Chapter 29

*DON'T OUTSHINE THE MASTER until you have your own Plantation.

In most cases out-shining the master (*at his place*) will have you headed for disaster and looking for a new master or plantation *regardless of how great you think you are*. There is a big difference between **"Productivity"** and being a *"Prima-Donna."* **Regardless of how *"Great or Valuable"* that you think you are, almost everybody is expendable**. If you have ideas or suggestions that you think could help improve a situation, present them in a proper forum, fashion & perspective so as **not to *"appear as if you are trying to come in and take over the program or run things"*** {even if this was your original plan, shun the appearance of evil and keep harmony in your situations. The harsh reality is that when you are working for someone else or some entity, they have you there for a reason, which most times are to produce, make money and make them look good. Whenever you are recognized for extraordinary feats or levels of productivity **never forget to give GOD the Glory, humble yourself and defer some of the credit to those that helped put you in position *Owners, General Managers, CEO's, Leaders or others* in addition to those that have helped you to be successful**. Remember that with Success in Life being a Team effort, the more you share your successes the more you will be Successful! Also remember that the acronym **T.E.A.M** stands for ***"Together Everybody***

Achieves More!" The moment that you begin to appear as if you are *"Bigger or Greater"* than the team, brand or organization that you represent is the moment they will begin to design your exit strategy. **Even though your performances & productivity will speak for itself, *tame your tongue* and only let *"blessings & praises"* come out of your mouth and refrain from evil communication**. They taught us in corporate America that if you're going to talk about someone that works there or in the same building or company that you need to be at least 3-5 miles away when you speak because ***"the walls have ears & tongues"*** .

*"**A listening ear can be a running mouth!"-** Monica Emery*

*****Special Note:*** *From my experience, it has been discovered that instead of being a **Superstar** where the focal point of the operation and all of the attention is focused on you and everything is about you , it's better to be a **Team-Player with Superstar Qualities** a situation where you are recognized as productive and your actions, talents & productivity speaks for itself in addition to **helping those around you to increase their talents & productivity to get better for the common good of the Team** which makes this situation **Mutually Beneficial**.*

Chapter 30

GAME TEST TO BRING OUT THE BEST: Never Expect What You Don't INSPECT!

"Test Everything"-1 Thessalonians 5:21

"Avoid every kind of evil"-1 Thessalonians 5:22

"It is better to trust in the Lord than to put confidence in man."-Proverbs 118:8

****Don't Expect What you don't Inspect!*** *Game-Test to Bring out the Best!* Always check important items going out to customers, clients & prospects by having a second person double check the items prior to shipping or delivery. *(People always act differently when they think you are watching them.* ***Create a "Checks & Balance" System*** *so that not only your business but everything that goes out of the door is double-checked for consistency, quality & clarity.* ***This can help to eliminate problems and reduce challenges before they occur.****) Know your personnel and keep in constant contact. If you are selling, promoting or marketing a product or service, test market it or try it for yourself or on yourself first so that you will understand the product or process and to make sure that you're not misrepresenting nor selling/ promoting a bad product or service.*

"Avoid every kind of evil"-1 Thessalonians 5:22

****Always know what's going on in all aspects of your business, financial & personal life + the current trends in your industry***. Regardless of the arena or entity, whether Military; Sports; Corporate America; Personal Relationships or Private Enterprise, you must "Game-Test" all applicants/prospects to show Position worthiness and Battle readiness. Prime example: In the military they have specialized training exercises, mock wars and battlefield simulation operations to gauge the quality of response, aptitude and performance. In sports they have what they call scrimmages against each other and against simulated opponents to evaluate talent & potential to operate under stress, duress and game like situations. In the school system they have fire drills. In the public sector they have tornado drills/air-raid sirens. In the media they have news-flashes/public-service announcements. In personal relationships you must "Game-Test" potential mates or applicants to make sure that they are not "star-struck" or" fair-weather fans" and in it for the long-haul & not just for short-term benefits or entertainment purposes.*

Special Note: *In interpersonal relationships* ***especially if you're not married*** most definitely make sure that you take extra measures to "***Never Assume: Inspect & Do Background Checks" and to "Protect Yourself at All Times!"*** *{Make sure that consent forms or waivers are signed, Use personal protection & check ID's.* The Life you save may be your own and **one *"Slip-Up"*** could result in wage garnishments +you paying a 20 year mortgage in support *or worse, a 20-year bid*!

"Before You Come out of Your Pocket with "Change", You better come out of your mouth with "Game" {as in "Game-Test" to make sure that it's the "Best!" - Big Ray

Chapter 31

*ALWAYS PLAY BY THE RULES!

"If you have to cheat to win, then you have already lost."

"Let all things be done decently and in order"-1 Corinthians 14:40

Always Play by the Rules** {unless you make the Rules, and if so, don't always make them up as you go! Play Fair.* ***Cheaters never prosper! If you don't feel like you can win, then don't get in! You Beat 50% of the people by working hard! You Beat 40% more by doing what's Right! The last 10% is a dogfight! Laws, Rules & Regulations were put in place for a Reason to maintain order & reduce chaos! If they are to be broken, amended or up-ended please use the proper forum or avenues to bring about a peaceful change.

*****Loop-holes are unnoticed, unannounced or seldom used exceptions or exemptions that are written or built into Laws, Rules & Regulations. Sometimes they come in the form of Grandfather clauses which means that they affect all entities that occur after or before a certain situations are in place. Other times they may be simply stated and just go unrecognized due to lack of knowledge of the***

Laws, Rules & Regulations set in place. This is why it's advisable to have someone with experience or wise counsel on your team that you can access for clarity, guidance, direction or correction in times of transition, disparity or confusion. In the event of legal issues, it is highly advisable to invoke your 5th amendment rights and keep your mouth shut and secure legal counsel/ representation or consult with a legal-aid society if you are income contingent to avoid being ensnared or trapped by the words of your mouth.

Chapter 32

*IF YOU CAN'T WIN, DON'T LOSE!

"Do Not Be Afraid to Walk Away from Mediocrity When it is an accepted practice and the majority present (& administration) is unwilling to change."

"You have to always put yourself in position to Win."-Big-E aka Coach Eric Jones

"You were not born Winners nor Losers, but Choosers!"-Devin Wyman

"Choose not to Lose! Winning is a Lifestyle!"-Big Ray

*"Somebody has to loose, but **it doesn't have to be YOU!"**-Big Ray*

"You might can't beat everybody, but Beat Somebody!"-Big Ray

"If you can't influence the outcome of a situation, then let it go. It's not for you to handle."-Marcellus Reed

Sometimes when operating in seemingly "*losing situations*" it may be easy to get weary, discouraged, lackadaisical or lack-luster in enthusiasm. A man once said;

"The worst bankrupt in the world is a man who has lost his enthusiasm!"

Keep the faith, stay strong and stay committed to the task at hand. Sometimes it's not always about the score at the end of the game, but more so about the energy, effort and resources utilized to compete in the event. ***Sometimes you win by not quitting and finishing the task or event?*** *Sometimes you win by improving performance & productivity from the beginning to the end while simultaneously setting the tone for future endeavors*. Sometimes you can win by *dominating and annihilating* your opponent, circumstances or situations. **Other times, Reality sets in and you realize that you are proverbially "*Beating a dead Horse*" or "*Riding a donkey in the Kentucky Derby*"** so to speak on your current project or placement and no matter how much effort you exhort it's not making a difference in productivity because the powers to be or associated with the project are unwilling or incapable of making a change for the better and you don't possess the authority to change or move them. This is when a Business decision has to be made. *Never set yourself up for failure*. **When it becomes evident that you are "*Riding a donkey in the Kentucky derby*", it's time to change stables and /or running mates, because *that's just a behind whipping waiting to happen.* You don't have to go down with the ship** (*contrary to popular belief*), **especially if it isn't yours. There are plenty more where they came from**.

"The same effort it takes to get to a row-boat or a dingy can be used to get to a yacht or a cruise ship"- Big Ray

Life is about Choices! You make some Good decisions and some not so good decisions and other times there are consequences and repercussions. Make conscientious choices and decisions that will put you in position to win {regardless of public opinion. Every battle is not yours and never enter into a battle, competition or contest where there are no spoils, Reward or chance of coming out Victorious!

"Somebody has to lose, but it doesn't have to be YOU! Choose Not to Lose!"-Big-Ray

Special Note: *Some people in some places/markets just don't want to win and will vehemently oppose you as well as despise you for the wisdom of your ways for trying to Win and bring about a positive change for the common good of the team or the community because Winning changes things and a lot of them are complacent with the status quo. When you begin to Win it will bring attention and shed a new light on your program that sometimes exposes inadequacies, hidden agendas or idiosyncrasies, nefarious activities, misconduct and/or wrong-doings (behind the scenes) of those associated or in leadership that previously went unnoticed with lower media coverage or fan participation. In addition,* ***Winning will sometimes cost extra that wasn't allocated or planned for***

***in the original budget**. A lot of people approach situations from a "fan" or a "consumer" point of view and fail to see the business perspective or the "administrative/ ownership" side of things. Example: If your favorite College football team makes it into the playoffs, most of the time they won't make money and will cause a deficit with all of the associated costs of performing in these events {travel, lodging, food, entertainment & more. Another example: If your favorite Pro-Football team makes it into the Playoffs and goes to or close to the Super-bowl, the Team-Owner will have to pay each individual player 45-man active roster + 7-10 man practice squad approximately $250k+ for each individual game past regular season in addition to performance bonuses & incentives that may be achieved with extra participation beyond regular season versus going 8-8 or having a .500 season, filling up their stadiums or arenas and making a profit.*

Be aware that these people do not want to be exposed, embarrassed or implicated on charges of misconduct or malfeasance of office and will go to great lengths to sabotage your program or plot your demise before they let that happen! *Just like Judas, they will claim to be with you and support you externally, while internally scheming & plotting to set you up for failure or take the fall on their behalf. That's why in some smaller markets they don't like "outsiders" because sometimes they not only see things for what they* *are, but also for what they could be and often times represent change, new energy & "New Beginnings!" From my vast experiences, I have seen instances of where an Administrator stole/purposely misplaced the Men's Basketball uniforms prior to the season and tried to make the players play in female uniforms which would subconsciously belittle, demean, demoralize, emasculate and distract the players from their goals & aspirations. In one stop along my journey, a group of seniors decided to throw the last game to avoid going to the playoffs because it would require them to practice in inclement weather and cut into their illicit activities off the field. At another stop in my journey, a Principal scolded our Head Coach for inspiring a young man to turn his life around, achieve Greatness and seek higher education, College or Trade-School after graduation from High School. The Principal told the Head Coach not to fill his head with such foolishness and that this particular young man wasn't "College or Trade-School material" even though he was an All-District Defensive Lineman and a pretty good mechanic and that he had him a job set up picking cotton on his farm after graduation. Our Head Coach inquired as to "what was our purpose for being there if we weren't going to teach, motivate & inspire the kids to Greatness, Higher Education or to get more out of life and take advantage of its opportunities?" The Principal replied that "everybody wasn't made for college" and that the player didn't have the aptitude and that he would end up flunking out and end up right back at home.*

In another situation along my many travels, an administrator informed our Head Coach that he had 5k in the budget to use for uniforms & equipment but after the Coach purchased some new helmets to upgrade the depleted & dilapidated inventory for safety purposes and to improve image & morale, he was told to slow down on purchases and after he ordered some new uniforms and had spent up to 2.5k of the budget, he was told to stop because the money was gone. When the Coach inquired as to what happened to it because he had receipts for all of his purchases and had only used half, the administrator indignantly replied (as if he didn't like being questioned or held accountable) that he had used it to repair the bus because we were going to need it for travel to away games even though we used a private contractor for transportation, paid for through the School Board. Never-the-less the writing was on the wall that we weren't going to be there too long. As a former team-mate of mine said when he was getting inducted into the Hall of Fame

*"**Begin with the end in mind**"-Aneas Williams*

When you enter into new situations, have your exit strategy available because all things in life are temporal or temporary and chances are that we will not be in one spot forever.

"Sometimes you have to change your atmosphere to change your year!"-Big Ray

"Sometimes in order to change your situation, you have to change your location or occupation!"-Big Ray

Special Note: *The same effort that it takes to make dimes in one market can be used to make Millions in another market that's fertile and receptive to your theories and thought processes.*

Chapter 33
ALWAYS OPERATE IN SUCCESS MODE INSTEAD OF STRESS MODE!

"Some people do what they want to do and others do what they have to do. ***This is the difference between "Stressful & Successful!****"-Big Ray*

"Always do the Best you can where you're at until you can get to where you want to be."-Octus Polk

"I don't do Vacation days, I do whenever I feel like it days!"-Lewis H. Williams

With the game of Life being 90% mental, always approach it with a positive mental attitude and a mindset to dominate, not just participate or ne a spectator. When faced with challenging situations, come with the mindset, appearance & approach of a Successful Victory!

The more you operate in Success mode, the more "*Successful*" you will be. Remember, that anything that you do for 21-days straight becomes a habit and that any habit duplicated for 40-days or more becomes a lifestyle. Pattern your lifestyle and mode of operations to that of being Successful instead of stressful. Tailor your atmosphere and surroundings to foster a Successful Spirit in the air. **Whenever you leave the house, go with an expectation of Success and Excellence!**

Chapter 34
BE A DIFFERENCE MAKER (PLAYMAKER)

"Greatness is not a Coincidence"!-Greg Wade

****Difference-Makers and/or Playmakers are often referred to as "Impact-Players", "Game-Changers" or known as an individual with the ability to change the game and /or your bank account as a single entity.*** By performing, producing and getting yourself placed into this category, *you now increase the demand for your products or services because you bring extra value to the table or team*. Imagine & visualize being a *"Barry Sanders, Barry Bonds, A-Rod, Wayne Gretzky or Michael Jordan"* of sorts in your field.

Next, **practice being Great over the next 21-days** by eliminating all bad habits, going above & far beyond the minimal acceptable standards by working hard, eating right and doing all the right things plus all of the little things that it takes to make your performance & productivity exceptional and stand out from all of the rest.

"If you want to be Great, you must do something extra!" -Coach Percy Duhe

{After practicing being Great for 21-days, being a difference maker is becoming a "Habit." From days 21-40 refine and *"fine-tune"* your game by taking it to another level to reach ***"elite-status."*** This stage of the game may prove to be challenging both mentally as well as physically. Not everybody reaches *"elite-status",* but you can if you put your mind to it. ***You need to have your mind, body and soul working in conjunction with one another*** during this transition stage. It is strongly suggested that during this time of transition to *"Greatness"* that you enrich your mind by studying up on your craft and by reading or searching extensively to improve your knowledge in your desired field of expertise. Maintain and/or increase your work-outs during this time period and continue consistently afterwards to improve endurance & strength. In addition, prayer time and spiritual enrichment is essential to reaching *"Greatness"* or *"elite-status"* because **nobody has ever achieved and maintained *"Greatness"* without GOD on their side**. Now that you have had *"Greatness"* in your Spirit for over 40-days, it now becomes a Lifestyle. It is up to you to keep it. Health & Wellness is essential if you are going reach *"Greatness"* or *"elite-status".* Make your Health a Priority, not a minority!

"You can't eat what everybody else eats and be elite!"-Big Ray

You need to refine and switch your diet up to include *"Premium"* or energy rich foods. **When you are going out to compete, act as if you are trying to win the Olympics**. *Eliminate foods & beverages that contain High fructose Corn Syrup, Refined Sugars, artificial sweeteners, bleached flour or High-sodium content because these can be the cause of cancer, diabetes, high-blood pressure and other ailments.* ***Stay off of Pork products****, processed foods & those high in sodium or sugar content when trying to compete or perform at ultimate levels.* Also cut down or limit red meat consumption prior to immediate competition because the prior aforementioned items can also make you *"sluggish"* or lethargic. Transition yourself to a 65% plant based or *"Mediterranean"* type of diet and educate yourself on the benefits of organic foods and alkaline water. The career and or life that you extend may be your own.

"If you fuel Rolls-Royce dreams with dime-store gas, you will eventually end up by the side of the road waiting on a tow truck*"-Big Ray*
www.MillionDollarSideHustle.com

Chapter 35

IF YOU'RE NOT NETWORKING, YOU'RE NOT WORKING!

NETWORKING & Recruiting People for your team:

"Your Network determines your Net-Worth!"

Turning Contacts into Contracts! Networking is meeting new people and being able to benefit or profit from these contacts. ***"Networthing" is being able to benefit, prosper and profit from these contacts on a consistent/continual basis*.** Put yourself in fertile places where networking is matriculating and growth oriented.

****People usually spend their money in 7-main areas: Church, Food, Hair, Clothing; Automobiles; Entertainment & Housing! Go where the $ goes & go where the $ grows.***

"You usually get what you get around. You can put on a 3-piece suit + nice shoes and go to work in a barn all day but when you come home, you will smell like horses & hay!"-Big-Ray.

If you're not networking, you're not working! If you don't prospect, it's harder to prosper. You need to incorporate at least 10-hours bare minimum into your schedule every week towards the guise of networking. As one of your "Success Habits" make it a point to give away at least 5-10 business cards or flyers on a minimum daily which will result in coming into contact with 150-300 new people/contacts/prospects monthly and 1500-3000 new contacts a year of which a certain percentage will subscribe to your theory/product or service. With Success in Life being a Team-Effort and a Numbers Game, this "Success Habit" will help you to reach your goals sooner than just sitting back and waiting on them to come to you. A prominent lady in the Hair industry once told me that "if you put out 1000 flyers a week, you will never go hungry!"

<u>Fertile Places to Network:</u>

***Golf-Courses & Driving Ranges** (also try some of the new indoor Golf & specialty places like Top-Golf)

***Gyms & Fitness Centers** (Especially chains like 24-Hour Fitness; Lifetime, LA-Fitness)

***Gas Stations/Convenience Stores** (QT/Quick-Trip gas stations, 7-Elevens; Circle-K's; Racetrack)

***Wal-Mart's, Sam's Clubs; Costco's; Grocery Store Chains** (Whole-Foods; Kroger; Tom Thumb; Albertson's),

***Happy Hours at popular Restaurants/Hotels in your city;** (Papadeaux, Houlihans, Dugan's; "W"-Hotels, The Omni, The Crowne Plaza, Radisson Hotels, Hilton Hotels; Sheraton Hotels; Embassy Suites; Renaissance Hotels.

***Little-League & High School Sporting Events, Games & Tournaments:** You will encounter mass amounts of people at these events, some of them there for chaperon purposes that are looking for something to occupy their mind until the event is over. One way to tap into the large base of fans that attend these events is to do "giveaways" of products, t-shirts or paraphernalia with your logo & marketing message on it. Another way is to hold drawing for free giveaways where they register/put their name into a drop-box, fish-bowl or ticket spinner. Don't overlook raffling off big-ticket items for $1-2 at these events and compiling data off of the ticket stubs.

<u>Compile a List/Database of Prospects, Recruits, Vendors, Customers, Clients & Associates:</u> Make sure that you secure the essential contact info: Proper Spelling of Name, Cell, Email, Mailing Address; Marital Status {name of spouse & kids if any), T-shirts size, favorite color, Birthday and any other demographic information pertinent to your business. As your business grows, this list will prove invaluable in the future.

<u>Special Note:</u> If you haven't figured it out yet, Life is about who you know, who knows you and to whom you are connected to, not necessarily all about what you can do {even though whatever you do, you should well or to the best of your ability.} Divine connection is the key to increase. The Lord will send people into your life for a Reason, a Season*

*or for a Lifetime. It is up to you to realize what their intent is in your life and fully utilize them to that extent. In essence, if anyone is experiencing lack or a shortage, they need to plug into "**The Power Source**" and a power source. If anyone is experiencing lack or a shortage, it's because of a lack of adequate preparation for the future and lack of adequate connection to "**The Power Source**" and a power source.*

Chapter 36
STAY 3-STEPS AHEAD OF THE GAME

"If you stay 1-step ahead of the game and slip & fall, when you get up you will be 2-steps behind. If you stay 3-steps ahead of the game, if you slip & fall, when you get up you're still a step ahead"-Big-Ray

Readers are Leaders and the reason why is because they are ahead of the game in reference to knowledge & application of that knowledge.

The Bible says that *"the people shall perish for a lack of knowledge..."* This passage hold true in various facets of life: Spiritual, Social, Physical, Financial, Business and Relationships.

As a player, coach, owner, manager, director or otherwise, learn what others (in your company) on your team do. It will well work to your advantage. Versatility will make you more efficient and effective as well as make you a more valuable asset to your team. In addition, it will also make you a greater threat to the competition because they don't know what area you are going to come from. Furthermore, in the event of downsizing, roster reductions or budget cuts, versatility will make you one of the last to be let go. If you are let go, it will make you one of the first to be hired/picked up elsewhere.

Be Creative. Always change your game plan periodically so that your opponent won't be able to predict your tendencies {from short & simple to complex & diverse and vice versa. Have balance. Be equally adept at doing all phases of whatever it is that you're doing i.e., running, catching, blocking, tackling; defense, offense, passing, shooting, rebounding.

Always Have a Back-Up {in everything: Game-plan, personnel, equipment, transportation, uniforms, financing. *{Depending upon climate, conditions & certain situations, change is inevitable. Being defeated is an option that you don't want to exercise."}* What is your "Plan-B"?

Use Wisdom & Logic: Work Smarter instead of Harder. Out think your opponent and develop a strategy & techniques that uses your opponent's strengths against them (i.e., Martial Arts, Judo, Wrestling, meditation, conditioning). The more experienced you are or the more experienced people you have the more you'll be able to accomplish in the long run.

Special Note: *Since most people in America are only a paycheck or two away from poverty even some of those who think that they have risen to affluence , save up the equivalent of 4-paychecks in your "Emergency-Contingency" fund for those times when life challenges happen & transition periods occur. In addition to this, for those of you who are self-employed, look at investing in a "Roth-IRA" and* *for those who work for others look at enrolling in your company's 501k program {especially those with company matching} and invest 10% per pay period. In the event of "lay-offs" or natural disasters you will be glad you did! You can never go wrong by wisely investing into your future.*

Chapter 37
NEVER UNDERESTIMATE AN OPPONENT!

In the military, they teach you to never underestimate an opponent based upon a visual perception. Sometimes things aren't always as they appear & may be camouflaged for security purposes or low-key visibility. Often times what appears to be easy prey may be an optical illusion designed to entrap or ensnare unsuspecting entities. Always be aware of the position of the enemy, adversary or opposition because they are always plotting your downfall or demise. You must be prepared for all phases of the game or the task at hand and it is advisable to stay 3-steps ahead of the game so that if you slip & fall, you can get back up and still be a step ahead. When in competition or at war, always keep you head on a "swivel" and anticipate deception and manipulation from your adversary or opponent because they want to put you out of business or commission.

"Always watch or be aware of who is watching you from the stands, because some of your biggest "frenemies" will be disguised as Fans!"

Special Note: *Judge your opponents not by their words, but by their actions.*

Chapter 38

DISCONNECT DISRESPECT FROM THE POWER SOURCE!

Sometimes you have to disconnect yourself from people emotionally in certain situations so that you can complete the task/job at hand. Never feed, give energy or power to a disrespectful individual or entity. By denying them access or cutting them off from your power supply *{& sometimes their own power supply}* you can now hinder/limit, ***dehydrate*** or ***starve*** off their ability to oppose you long term. Most of the times that you encounter disrespect; it will derive from a *"Lack of knowledge; education, experience, etiquette, sportsmanship or familiarity with the terrain/ arena or rules of the game of which the offending party is operating in."* Whether you choose to deal with this act directly, indirectly or subcontract to an *"outside"* source, this incident must be dealt with to discourage this mistake from reoccurring. Various methods can be applied to send a message or take a stand from verbal, non-verbal, physical, mental, financial, deletion of privileges or communication access for the offending party. If this situation goes unaddressed or is not dealt with accordingly, the offending party will think that this act of disrespect is an acceptable form of behavior and will escalate this behavior or have others performing these "*heinous*" acts. Sometimes in life you have to set an example and other times, *"You have to make an Example to discourage foolishness in the future!"* Just like a puppy dog that has pooped in the wrong place, corrective action needs to be taken and whichever method that you choose is totally up to you? Whether you choose to have a conversation about it to "*hit them in the head with some knowledge*" or proverbially rub their noses in it, put the newspaper to their behind, put them outside or in solitary confinement or hit them in the pocket to give them something they can feel, the remedies are endless.

Special Note: ***Do not put people in a position of where they will feel comfortable disrespecting you because they think they're exempt from "consequences & repercussions." Prevention is better than the cure. "If you don't see them in your future, then why are they in your presence?"-Big Ray***

*****Special Note:*** ***Avoid Intimate & Business Relationships with those who do not respect you, your time and "your dime" or see your vision!*** *The wrong people who are in your life don't always leave voluntarily. Sometimes you have to cut the strings and sever the ties! Other times you have to **"Punt"** or give them the proverbial boot to get out of a hole or a rut, reposition and get better field position. Self-preservation is essential!*

Chapter 39

BE ON TIME OR BEFORE TIME!

"Time is a Valuable Commodity when once lost, can never be regained! Use it wisely!"-Big Ray

"The early bird catches the worm, the rest catch the germs. (You can't fish with germs, but with a worm, you can catch the fish that got away."

In sports as well as in life, proper timing is essential. It not only sets the tone for completing assignments and reaching the finish line first, but it is also a sign of discipline, respect and proper etiquette as well. Besides, it makes it harder for someone to set you up for failure if you arrive to places early or before time.

Proper time utilization helps to prepare adequately & eliminate mistakes or accidents caused due to rushing or lack of preparation. There are 24-hours in a day. Set a schedule that will encompass all 24-hours and include times to work, play, and worship & pray {+workout. In this schedule set times for nutrition & hydration breaks, rest, family, fitness & finances.

In other facets of life, such as the work place, it could be construed as a sign of honesty as in a day's work for a day's pay. Imagine if you were an employer and you had a worker that you employed at a rate of $40 an hour and they showed up 15 minutes late twice a month? Now imagine if this same employee came back from lunch once a month 15 minutes late & left once a month 15 minutes early on a Friday? The average consumer wouldn't see any harm or foul in this with the common excuses of traffic jams/accidents, had to pick up/drop off kids or inclement weather. *{When I played football, they taught us that if we weren't Dead, In Jail or the Hospital or at a Funeral, we were supposed to be there on time or before time with on-time being late!}*

Now look at this same equation from the view of a Producer or a Business owner if you will? **To a small Business owner if 10 employees embraced this same philosophy that would equate to a loss of approximately $4,800 a year + a loss of 120 man hours of productivity a year! To a Medium-Large Business owner, if 100 workers operated in this fashion it would equate to a loss of $48,000 in wage expenses + a loss of 1200 man hours of productivity a year.**

Now let's sum it up from a Consumer's perspective. If someone took $480-$4,800 out of your bank account/paycheck over a year's time, you would want to fight & call the police, authorities or the Equal Employment Opportunity Commission to file robbery, theft or fraud charges.

Special Note: *My father had taught me to always give people value for their money and to never try to get over or beat anybody out of their money when it came to business transactions. Give people what* *they pay for and meet, beat or exceed their expectations to get ahead instead of giving just bare minimum. The same holds true when it comes to preparing for sports or competition.*

Chapter 40

THE GOLDEN RULE

***Remember: The Golden Rule!** In elementary or pre-school you were lead to believe that the Golden Rule meant to do unto others as you would have them do unto you in order to create a cooperative atmosphere of peace, order, tranquility and non-violence toward others. Fast-forward years later to post-adolescence; where you start experiencing the "Real-World" that is "Cold, Cruel & Cut-throat" with chaos and not so nice actions going on which brings out the true revelation of the meaning of this term. {Treat others like they need to be treated according to their actions & productivity and to remember that he who has the gold, rules.*

Chapter 41
RESPECT THE GAME (& Your Elders)

"Those who don't Respect the Game will wreck the game!"

In all facets of life you should respect your elders and submit to authority and leadership *{as long as they are leading in the right direction}*, whether it is the policeman in the street, the Teacher in the classroom, The Judge in the court, The Preacher in the Church, The Coach on the field or the Supervisor on the job.

"The future that you create will be determined by the instructions that you follow"-Mike Murdock

Promotion comes from doing your job well, your ability to follow instructions and being respectful as well as loyal & obedient to those whom you serve. Demotion or *"deletion"* comes when you disrespect, disobey or disregard laws, rules, regulations, orders, instructions or commands from those who rule over you.

"A person who can't take or receive instructions may be headed for self-destruction or roster reduction!"

"Egos & Selfishness are the recipes for disaster"-William Baker

"Obedience is better than Sacrifice..."-1 Samuel 15:22

When you perform a job or a service, *"Take Ownership"* and perform the task as if you owned the company and it was a reflection of you or do it to the best of your ability the way you would want to be served or serviced if you were a customer, client, supervisor or Coach.

In order to become a Great Leader, you must be "*Coachable & Teachable*" + willing to follow orders, perform well or do *"Exceptionally & Exceedingly above all others"* that which you will want done for you or on your behalf in the future. The best leaders are those who have experienced what those they are leading have went through and can relate to trials and that may sometimes go along with the task or job at hand in addition to being able to advise how to overcome adversity and obstacles that may come along with the job or assignment.

Respect comes in many forms such as Responsibility, Accountability & Discipline {in addition to courtesy, good sportsmanship, law abiding citizenship, manners, etiquette, wardrobe, attitude, effort & motivation plus many other facets of life. Respect is a sign of discipline, good character traits and leadership qualities.

"If as coaches we embrace the calling, we must accept the responsibility of being the best coach, teacher and role model possible"-Bobby Bowden

Just as we mentioned in an earlier chapter as to how image was important, you also need to consider the images & reputations of those that you align yourself with to make sure that it's a right fit. Just because a person or an entity is extremely attractive, talented, gifted or financially secure in a particular area doesn't necessarily mean that they are a good fit for you or your team. In the bible it refers to passages about being equally/un-equally yoked, using wisdom and the value of a good name. In sports, business and personal relationships you have to do a background check and check their resume/references before letting them on your team or getting into business/bed with a new individual or entities. One mistake in this area can be the cause of major setbacks and headaches of which could cost more to get out of than the originally anticipated outcome or payoff. ***Avoid Intimate & Business Relationships with those who do not respect you, your time, and "your dime" or see your vision!*** The wrong people who are in your life don't always leave voluntarily. Sometimes you have to cut the strings & sever the ties! Other times you have *to* ***"Punt"*** or give them the proverbial boot to get out of a hole or a rut, reposition and get better field position. Self-preservation is essential! GOD sends people into our lives for a Reason, a Season or a Lifetime! It is up to us to discern what their purpose is and fully utilize it to that extent. Everybody you meet can do at least 2-things for you? It is up to you to determine what those 2-things are {either get with the program or Scram.

Chapter 42
ALWAYS HAVE A GAME-PLAN AT HAND!

"Failure is often the result of ignoring GOD! He does not like to be excluded from our planning."

"Commit to the Lord whatever you do and He will establish Your Plans"-Proverbs 16:3

"GOD must be in the mix or else we will fail."

"Follow a Plan and not a Man"

If you don't have a plan, you can plan to fail. Do not rely on "*Luck.*" ***Luck is when preparation meets opportunity.*** Prior preparation prevents poor performance. Establish ***what it is that you are trying to achieve?*** Qualify this goal by asking yourself the following questions: "***is it obtainable & maintainable***" and "***what does it take to make it happen?***" *Am I willing to do what it takes to obtain this goal* and *am I willing to do what it takes to maintain after achieving this goal*?

"Everyone has the dream. To make your dream a reality you need the plan, the process, the people, the persistence, the patience, and the passion."-Jeffrey Gitomer

Game-planning or setting a Strategy is a Blueprint for Success! Develop a blueprint, pattern or diagram to achieve your goals. In this blueprint or pattern, ***describe how you will solve problems, provide value & reward for your team or prospective***

clients (because you will receive no reward until you do so. Success & $ is a reward you receive when you solve problems for others.) Make sure that your plan answers the following questions: Who, what, when, where, how & why?

"If it doesn't solve problems, make dollars, save money or time, it doesn't make sense and if you don't have any, how much is your opinion worth?"- Big Ray

Special Note: *The main reason you buy this book and get a plan is because* ***"neither Championships nor Money comes with instructions!"*** *It's a tool that you can use and an element of exchange, but you need to use it wisely. Even though it's made out of trees, it doesn't grow on trees unless you have a tree farm . You can acquire it, but if you don't know what to do with it or have a plan in hand or in place it can get misplaced into the wrong hands. You've heard the old saying "If you fail to plan, you can plan to fail." Same thing can happen with "Your Championship" & your money if you don't have a plan for it. Other people have plans for your Championships & your money when you don't, because it's a magnet and it attracts all kinds! You don't want certain people, leeches, vermin or liabilities in your circle or on your team.*

"A fool & his money are soon departed."

"Wisdom is the principal thing; therefore get wisdom and with all thy getting, get understanding"-Proverbs 4:7

Learn to regulate your outcomes & cash flow, so that cash flow & outcomes don't regulate you.

Chapter 43

IF IN DOUBT, CALL A TIME-OUT!

"And He said unto them, Come ye yourselves apart into a desert place and rest a while: for there were many coming and going, and they had no leisure so much as to eat"-Mark 6:31

When life's challenges arise and sometimes you don't have an answer in sight, do not be afraid to pause efforts and "Call a Time-Out" to regroup and game-plan on your current situation. A lot of people have a *"Full-Steam ahead" or "Always go at 100% or 100 miles an hour"* philosophy but *for those times when you find yourself in a proverbial hole, stop digging and start climbing!* Some challenges in life are latitude which means going the distance and or finishing the race. Other times challenges may appear in the form of altitude which will require you to go to different heights or levels to overcome obstacles or the task at hand. This is where "Time-outs" come in handy. It gives you time to utilize principles of *"The Laws of Recognition"* to recognize/realize what obstacle that you are up against and set an adequate game plan to achieve your goals. If your obstacle is a vertical challenge, it may be ludicrous to run around in circles or long distances for miles when you need to reach greater heights to achieve your goal and vice versa to jump up & down, climb walls or mountains if it's a horizontal challenge.

Chapter 44

LIFE IS ABOUT CHOICES
{It's hard to go wrong doing the Right Thing!

"...no good thing will He withhold from them who walk uprightly."-Psalm 84:11

"You are what you repeatedly do. Excellence therefore is not an act, but a habit"-Aristotle

*"People do not decide to become extraordinary. They **decide to accomplish extraordinary things.**"-Edmund Hillary*

In life you will make some good decisions and some not so good decisions and often times, there will be consequences and repercussions. Being challenged in life is inevitable. Being defeated is optional. **Choose not to Lose!** Make good sound decisions that always put you in a position to Win! If you're not winning, go back to the beginning and then come forward step by step to determine where you went wrong & what was done wrong so that you may correct your mistakes and not make the same mistakes over & over. In the sports world we were taught that "***the biggest mistake is to continue to practice making a mistake once it has been discovered that a mistake has been made.***" I have seen various instances of where people have discovered mistakes being made and continue on as if nothing happened and figure that the mistakes will correct themselves or they will deal with them at a later time? I've seen instances in football where one team was committing a mistake against an opponent and the overall consensus of the coaching staff was that we will fix it next week in practice instead of calling a time-out and getting a better understanding among the players & coaches of how to rectify & correct the situation when it was discovered. The way to win consistently is to eliminate errors or mistakes and not to repeat them over and over which is why we tell people to ***"Choose not to Lose!"***

Correct your actions and/ or mistakes then take measures to make sure that these actions never reoccur because **a "*Mistake*" committed more than once is a DECISION.**

"The Biggest mistake is to continue to make a mistake once it has been realized that a mistake has been made".

"There is a way which seemeth right unto man, but the end thereof are the ways of death." Proverbs 14:12

"A Mistake committed more than once is a decision!"

<u>Special Note:</u> "You beat 50% of the people by working hard! You beat 40% more by doing what's Right! The last 10% is a Dog-Fight!"

Chapter 45
WHEN CHOOSING A MATE, MAKE SURE THAT YOU EVALUATE:
What are they bringing to the Table?

RELATIONSHIPS: *"Are you Qualified to be $atisfied?"-Big-Ray*

"Never confuse Relationships with Situation-ships"-Pastor Freddie Haynes.

"Everybody you meet can do at least 2-things for you? It is up to you to determine what those 2-things are?"-Penny St. James.

"A lot of people want to win, but don't want to do what it takes to WIN!"-Big-Ray

"Don't give quality time to unqualified people"-Charisse L.Brown

"Can they cook a meal or close a deal?"-Snoop Dogg's Character in Bossin-Up

"Are they eligible to be elevated"-Big Ray

Relationships are a process of exchange. The key word for the day is "Mutually Beneficial", which means that all parties involved should benefit from the Relationship{not necessarily equally because sometimes others will have more to invest or loose depending on the level of investment. There are 3-parts to a Relationship: *The Physical, Financial & Communication.* Of these 3, *Communication* is the most important because the first 2 can leave you at any moment. In any good relationship there must be good D.I.C. Dollars, Information & Contacts. You must determine which of these that you are bringing to the table & which of these that you need? If you possess none of these, you need to reassess your vision then go and align yourself with some people that can help you to achieve and/or acquire your goal. Sometimes in life when you are lacking in Resources/ D.I.C. Dollars, Information & Contacts it may be necessary to team with others for a few seasons to help them achieve their goals/aspirations to learn the system or become acclimated with others who can fuel-inject your project. The acronym ***TEAM stands for: Together Everybody Achieves More***. Now a-days, you hear the buzz-word **"Team-Player"** being utilized a lot. Do not be dismayed nor *led astray* by this term. *In corporate America we were taught that being a "Team-Player" comes about after one completes their own responsibilities to themselves.* "To thine on self be true, and then you can be true to your friends." In this quest of excellence, you must have: Character, Integrity and Principles especially in terms of Relationships.

The "5-C's of Relationships. When gathering data to determine if you are going to move forward into a new relationship, always check for the "5-C's" which are: **Christ, Car, Crib, Credit and Career.**

Take inventory of how a potential new prospect grades out in each area and tabulate their score.

(Scoring System: Just as in the educational system you were graded out on test scores and aptitude to see if you would be promoted to the next grade level, you should grade out applicants in the relationship department to see if *"they're eligible to be elevated"* or that you want to promote them to the next level. Scoring Ratings: **C-70-79 % Just a Friend/Associate; B-80-89 % Potential Business Liaison/Dating Prospect; A-90%+= Potential Business Partner/Mate or Spouse.** (Anything or anyone that scores below "C" level needs to go back for remedial studies and polish up their game a bit before trying out for your team/organization. Remember, it takes more to be a Champion! If you don't set *"Standards"* or have *"Criteria"* for membership on your team, you will be in for the biggest disappointment since you found out that there was *"No Santa Claus."*

"Be careful of whom you choose to date... A lot of people ain't looking for LOVE, they're looking for HELP."-Comedian Anastasia The Bold

The "3-B's of Relationships: Other attributes to take into account when contemplating on entering into potential new relationships are: **Brains, Bank & Business Sense.** Pre-screening applicants for these attributes will help to alleviate many future headaches, heartaches and strife in addition to reducing tension and anxieties.

Never Defecate and Eat in the same Place! There is a time, a place and a Season for everything.

Just as you don't eat Dinner in the Bathroom, nor defecate & urinate in the Kitchen, Refrain from developing or engaging in interpersonal relationships within the workplace (unless it's a family business or mutually agreed to in advance to make it official by both parties involved.) Reason being is that not only can this cause both parties that are involved to lose focus/productivity but also can negatively affect the focus & productivity of associates, co-workers and constituents as well. Not only that, but when the time comes to dissolve such relationships, they usually cause division, tension, stress and strife in the work place and could result in you seeking employment opportunities or employees elsewhere.

Pre-Screening for Future Potential:

"When you first meet someone, check out their hair, feet, hands & nails {+teeth}. If they can't take care of them, they can't take care of you!"-Angie Hamlin

Just as we mentioned in an earlier chapter as to how image was important, you also need to consider the images and reputations of those that you align yourself with to make sure that it's a right fit.

"Do not be misled/ deceived: Bad company corrupts good Character"-*1Corinthinans 15:33*

Just because a person or an entity is extremely attractive, talented, gifted or financially secure in a particular area doesn't necessarily mean that they are a good fit for you. In the bible it refers to passages about being equally/un-equally yoked, using wisdom and the value of a good name. In business and personal relationships you have to do a background check and check their resume/references before getting into business/bed with a new individual or entities. One mistake in this area can be the cause of major setbacks and headaches of which could cost more to get out of than the originally anticipated outcome or payoff of the initial product offering.

"It's better to be alone that in the presence of Bad Company or companions!"

Avoid Intimate & Business Relationships with those who do not respect you, your time, and "your dime" or see your vision!

When contemplating entering into new interpersonal relationships have a pad with at least 25+ or more qualities listed that you are looking for in a mate then grade out/pre-screen new applicants on a percentage basis of how they stack up against your list to eliminate wasting your time, their time or your dime! (If you didn't have at least 20-25 preferred qualities listed, you didn't give it much considerable thought & go back and think thoroughly. They should grade out at 70% or more to be your friend; 80% or more to be a girlfriend/boyfriend & 90% or better for marriage material.)* ***Nobody is perfect, but there is someone perfect for you!* *This eliminates having* *to go through 9 or 10 candidates just to find out number 3 was the right one!*

The wrong people who are in your life don't always leave voluntarily. Sometimes you have to cut the strings & sever the ties! Other times you have to "Punt" or give them the proverbial boot to get out of a hole or a rut, reposition yourself and get better field position. Self-preservation is essential! GOD sends people into our lives for a Reason, a Season or a Lifetime! It is up to us to discern what their purpose is in our lives and fully utilize it to that extent. Everybody you meet can do at least 2-things for you? It is up to you to determine what those 2-things are.

Chapter 46
NEVER DISCUSS YOUR PROBLEMS WITH THOSE INCAPABLE OF A SOLUTION!

"Sometimes a listening ear can be a running mouth."-Monica Emery

Never receive counsel from unproductive people nor discuss problems with those incapable of contributing to the solution. Watch where you get your advice and check your sources for validity.

"If you complain about what you're going through, it's hard to focus on where you're going to!"-Devin Wyman

Whenever you face problems, obstacles or adversity in life, you need to first search within to see if you can discover an adequate solution or path to achieve your goals. If unable to come up with an adequate solution, we recommend going to a Professional Problem Solver. Pray to GOD, talk to Jesus and seek the Holy Spirit for Wisdom, Guidance & Knowledge to overcome any obstacle that may come before you. Next, consult wise counsel and/or a competent experienced mentor to Coach, teach/ instruct and guide you on your path towards Greatness. If your problem is spiritual, seek spiritual guidance of a seasoned Pastor or Spiritual Leader. If your problem is financial, find a financial advisor *whose salary or compensation is not based upon the information that they give to you.* If you are experiencing health related issues, then consult with a personal trainer and a health care professional and not necessarily one that wants to load you up on pharmaceuticals to mask the problem but more so one that wants to get to the root cause of the problem and help you to eradicate it naturally whenever possible. When you encounter legal issues, consult with a licensed attorney, (legal aid society or paralegal if your finances don't allow) to give you an accurate interpretation of your options and potential outcomes. Stay away from *"hearsay and street-level chatter"* because in the court of law, *"ignorance is no excuse!"* If your issue happens to be sports related, get or acquire you at least 3-gurus or retired Coaches or Athletic Directors (on Speed-Dial) that were known to be Great or Good at what they do. Sometimes when problems or obstacles arise, what appears to be a mountain to some may seem to be a mole-hill or ant pile to others. It's not always what you know or whom you know, but more so to whom you are connected to and who knows you. You need to be connected and have access to information. The Bible states that *"My people are destroyed for lack of knowledge"-Hosea 4:6*

"Sometimes it's not the amount of times that you try, but it's the means by which one is willing to go through to reach their objective"-Big Ray

Special Note: *When seeking advice make sure that you don't divulge too much pertinent information about your issue until you are sure that you have secured the right source and that they can assist you in addition to keeping your information confidential. Your information falling into the hands of an opponent or adversary can have adverse effects and be counterproductive.* ***(Sometimes it's good to have people sign non-disclosure, non-compete; memorandum of understanding or confidentiality clauses before going into deep detail about sensitive issues that can affect your livelihood.)***

Chapter 47

ADAPT AND ADJUST YOUR GAME TO FIT THE TERRAIN

"Never make a Long-Term decision based upon a temporary situation!"

"When you're born or operating in a jungle, there is no such thing as "Crawl before you walk?' You have about 15-18 minutes to get it together when you exit the womb, and then you have to hit the ground running or get left behind!"-Big Ray

"Self-Preservation is a Number-1 Priority!"-Big Ray

"Being Challenged in Life is inevitable. Being defeated is Optional!"-Roger Crawford

"You must either modify your dreams or magnify your skill"-Jim Rhon

Anticipate that there will be obstacles along your journey towards "Greatness" that will have to be solved or overcome in order for you to reach and achieve your Goals & Objectives. Due to the competitive nature of Life, you will mainly encounter 4-types of people and you will have to figure out which one are you: *Those who make things happen; those who watch things happen, those that wonder what happened & those that things happen to!*

I grew up in the Midwest in Detroit, Michigan aka *"The Murder-Capital of the World"*

"Where the Strong Survive and the rest get eaten alive!"

It was a nice place to go shopping for cars, suits & shoes, but you did not want to live there. Growing up we learned fast that in order to be successful; you had to be able to overcome obstacles quick and to ***"adapt & adjust your game to fit the terrain***". *Not only did we have to deal with the elements The 4-Seasons , but We Had to Deal with "The-Elements" Day-to-day Survival/Staying Alive! For most residents, operating in "Fear"* ***False Evidence Appearing Real was*** not an option if you planned on staying? For those who did, their future was not in Detroit. Close encounters with Bully's, Robbers, Muggers, Thugs, and Thieves & Con-men were commonplace even in the more affluent areas of town. You couldn't always run from it unless you relocated to another state and sometimes they still came and found you because a lot of times you would encounter the same problem the next day in your daily commute or on your journey to school. As the singer Kenney Rogers stated & sang in the movie *The Gambler:*

"You have to know when to hold them, know when to fold them, know when to walk-away and know when to Run! "

(In my family, the only time running from people or your problems were acceptable was in the case of someone shooting at you or bullets flying. Other than that, you had to handle your business or you were going to get the Business!)

At a very early age, we developed gifts of discernment, networking, assessment and problem solving skills in addition to learning how to barter, communicate & negotiate! Tasks that seem simple to most such as going to school or to the store to pick up items for your parents were challenging and required a certain degree of preparation (Like going to war.) I've heard several stories of kids getting sent to the store (or school) & getting jumped or robbed in the process and returning home empty-handed or minus an article of clothing or shoes. Once their parent or guardian got wind of the situation, they would give them a *"motivational speech"*, sometimes a whipping and a set of instructions along with cash & tools to complete the task or rites of passage and told not to return to the house without the items they were sent for or with. *(Back in those days, the only acceptable excuse for coming home empty-handed was if someone pulled a gun on you or was shooting at you!)* It's a Jungle out there and Situations such as these cause you to mature at a rapid rate and come up with solutions to problems that present themselves in a matter of minutes, sometime seconds to alleviate having to deal with a larger problem later on. *"Imagine being young and experiencing a robbery/mugging then being faced with the possibility of homelessness if you didn't retrieve the lost items?"* This would definitely put you in a different frame of mind! You find out quick how to win/ beat someone or alleviate problems and incorporate it into your game-plan. The 9-main ways that you beat an opponent is to:

#1-HAVE GOD ON YOUR SIDE;

#2 Overpower them Dominate Your Opponent and annihilate their will to win.

#3 Out-Quick them Run-Faster, Get the jump on them/Be First or Beat them to the Punch.

#4 Out-Think them Strategy/Come up with a Better Game-Plan than theirs or find their weakness and exploit it.

#5 Out-Last them Endurance/You're in Better Shape or able to withstand the conditions longer than they can. *"You'll Win if You Don't Quit!"*

#6 The Element of Surprise-"Catch Them Slipping, Sleeping or Leaking" Sometimes when and opponent doesn't respect you or see you as a potential threat to defeat them, they will get lackadaisical, sloppy or complacent with the status-quo and let their guards down which would make that a prime time for a counter-attack.

#7 **Join Them** *"Sometimes if you can't beat them, join them"* Sometimes you have to infiltrate an opponent's camps, study and scout them out to determine what their mindset, theories, strengths, weaknesses , common enemies, common allies and utilize this information to your best benefit.

Other times, if you can't beat them "Hire Them." Some people are just good at what they do and are a technician or master of the game. With you wanting the Best possible Team, Product or Service available, why not tender an offer to that adversary that has proven to be a major challenge or stumbling block in your path or pursuit of Excellence. Sometimes, what the competition/ opposition was doing wasn't personal, just business and if this is the case, tendering an offer that they can't refuse will help to overcome a challenge in addition to improving productivity in just one move. Sometimes grass can be greener on the other side of the fence if the right seeds are planted, watered and fertilized.

#8 Relocate to an area or environment where the adversary would become inefficient or ineffective.

"Sometimes in order to change your situation, you have to change your location or occupation!"-Big Ray

"Sometimes in order to change your year, you have to change your atmosphere!"-*Big Ray*

Every challenge in life doesn't always have to be a *"Battle or a War"*. Sometimes it works better to *"think smarter instead of harder."* Just as in business Location plays an important part, proper positioning can not only serve useful in marketing, branding and promotional terms but be a major security mechanism as well. Just as in the scientific arena where *Geography determines growth*, or even the plant & animal kingdom where certain organisms needs certain elements, climate or type of environment in order to survive or feel comfortable, the same holds true with the opposition. Prime examples; fresh water fish don't do well in salt water & vice versa; certain fruits & vegetables don't grow well or go bad in certain climates; certain animals or mammals can't survive well at lower depths of the sea without proper protection or a pressure suit because of the variances of air pressure at certain depths; when you go up the side of a mountain, they have a snake line. Snakes can't survive at higher altitudes because of the atmospheric pressure on their brain. *In retrospect, "Let your next move be your best move like a chess move!" A simple move up the mountainside, into the suburbs or the countryside can not only reduce the confusion or competition but sometimes create a position of attractiveness, affluence and of a monopoly{which depending on the type of business that you are in + the supply & demand for your product or services is not always a bad thing.*

#9 Eliminate or Neutralize the Threat Sometimes in Life as in Business you have to put opponents out of business or into early retirement *legally or through fair competitive practices* or rearrange their focus to things that are more important than competing with you! Very Important: Before you try using this measure use Wisdom and don't be Greedy, it's enough out here for everybody. *Everybody plays an important part in* *the ecosystem*. If you eliminate all competitors this would create a situation of a monopoly after which would make you a target and sooner or later someone will try to use this measure on you? *(There is more than one way to skin a cat!) Besides, there has to be somewhere for the people to go that you don't want on your team or that you don't want subscribing to your products & services. (If it wasn't for the Washington Generals, the Harlem Globetrotters rise to fame might have been a steeper climb.)*

Dealing with the elements: When I was a Boy Scout, our motto was "Always Be Prepared!" Growing up in the Midwest we encompassed all 4-seasons of weather that included snow, ice, rain, heat, fallen leaves, strong-winds & tornados. When the seasons changed, we changed and or adapted to fit the terrain that came with each new season. At the end of August we might me wearing Bermuda short & tank tops. By the 3rd week of September you had better have a windbreaker, sweater or light jacket available to fight of the brisk winds of autumn approaching. Entering into the 2nd or 3rd week of November when the cold fronts were more prominent we started breaking out with the dress boots, mid-weight coats & jackets. When December arrived, it was time to break out the snow boots & ski suits along with the heavyweight parkas and overcoats. Towards the end of March –the middle of May it was time to break out the active "Rain-gear.'

June signaled the time to break out your lightweight linens and open toe shoes or sandals.

In the Sports World sometimes we would be going up against a formidable opponent that had very talented athletes and still had to find a way to accomplish our goals and come out victorious.

"It's not the amount of times that you try, but more so the means by which one is willing to go through to reach their objective!"

Our mission was to get their star players (or difference makers) to lose focus and turn their attention span to something other than winning against us by any means necessary. Some of the tactics used to accomplish this task were mental such as silly prank phone calls the night before the game, orchestrated chants or talking trash to an opponent before, during and in between plays. Other tactics were physical such as "Gang-tackling" an opponent and hitting them extra hard under the pile or setting hard picks, fouls or screens.

In the Business world sometimes we run specials, discounts & give-a ways or somewhat slanderous commercials to get opponents/competitors to lose focus.

From my observations and experiences, one of the quickest ways an opponent would lose focus was in the event of "Pain!"

"Pain changes the Game!"-Big-Ray

"The Quickest Way to get defeated is to become Distracted!"

Pain can come in many shapes and forms: Physical, Mental & Financial.

"Your ability to deflect pain, inflict pain and withstand pain will sometimes determine the height of your accomplishments."-Big-Ray

"Everybody has a plan until they get hit!"-Mike Tyson

Sometimes in life in order to repel an opponent or an adversary you have to administer a "blow" *or message* so shocking, intense and convincing that your adversary will have to reevaluate and refocus their reasons for competing against or trying to suppress your efforts in the first place? *(When you deliver this blow it has to be with a high-level of intensity so that your opponent is "**Convinced**" that you are not the one to be toyed with! Now whether you decide to deliver this message to their mind, behind or bank-account or all 3-at the same time is up to you! If you come with anything less than intense this method will back-fire and you should prepare to receive a barrage of retaliation!)*

Choose Not to Lose! "Winning is a Lifestyle!"

*The moral to the stories are that sometimes situations & circumstances force you to adapt & adjust to overcome obstacles, challenges & fears to find a way to survive or Win!

***Special Note**: **Keep things in proper perspective!** *Stories mentioned in this book are for illustration & motivation purposes only!* ***Do not misconstrue the contents of this book or the intentions of the author as those of inciting illegal activity or violence towards another human being! Life is a Precious Gift from GOD! Do whatever you can to preserve and enjoy it while it last**! Self-Preservation is a Number-1 Priority!*

{As they say in the Boxing World, "Protect Yourself at All Times!"} Regardless of your situation or circumstances all things in life are temporal/temporary and ***you can Win if You Don't Quit!*** *Find the Champion up above & within, because "Winners Always Find a Way to Win &* ***CHAMPIONS FIND A WAY TO WIN THE BIG ONE!"***

Chapter 48

DARE TO BE GREAT! PRACTICE WHAT YOU PREACH! Always finish STRONG and Thank GOD for His Blessings & Opportunities.

"I would rather be hated for Greatness instead of being liked for lameness in my Game!"-Big Ray

"You don't have to be Great to get started, but you do have to get started to be Great!"-Devin Wyman

"As a Coach, it's not what you know, but what you teach"-Grant Teaff

"Greatness is not a Coincidence!" –Greg Wade

"I was once told not to bite off more that I could chew; I said that I would rather choke on Greatness rather than nibble on mediocrity!"

"People do not decide to become extraordinary. They decide to accomplish extraordinary things."-Edmund Hillary

"You are what you repeatedly do. Excellence therefore is not an act, but a habit"-Aristotle

The Best way to Lead is by Example. You have a lot of so-called *"leaders"* that will ask you to perform, execute and achieve extraordinary feats or tasks but yet were unwilling to perform the same requests when put in your position. Never ask someone to do that of which you would be unwilling to do unless you're paying them for their services or hiring a Professional***. Remember that someone is always***

watching you regardless of what level that you may think that you're on and that you're are constantly under surveillance even in closed quarters. If you are Coaching, Teaching or Preaching Excellence, then **Excellence should be exemplified.** It should be in your walk, your talk and your actions consistently. If you're extolling the bad effects of drugs & alcohol to your team or students; then set a good example and don't be a *closet "wine-o", "junkie" or "weed-head".* If your message to the congregation is to flee fornication, then don't have 5 or 6 women on the side. Now, with that being said, we are all human and prone to error. If you have a fall, get back up, clean yourself off and correct your actions and/ or mistakes then take measures to make sure that these actions never reoccur because a *"Mistake"* committed more than once is a DECISION. The way to win consistently is to eliminate errors or mistakes and not to repeat them over and over which is why we tell people to *"Choose not to Lose!"*

"The Biggest mistake is to continue to make a mistake once it has been realized that a mistake has been made."

A lot of the Blessings and Opportunities that we receive are a Privilege, (not a Right) and not to be taken lightly. **In the grand scheme of things almost everybody is expendable.** Always Thank GOD for what you have and claim the increase because **Rights & Privileges can and sometimes will be revoked and taken away.**

"Give thanks in all circumstances for this is GOD'S will for you in Christ Jesus"-1 Thessalonians 5:18

<u>ABC'S OF WINNING!</u>

***ALWAYS TAKE GOD WITH YOU AND USE YOUR MIND:** *"The Game is 90% Mental".*

"Commit to the Lord whatever you do and He will establish Your Plans"-Proverbs 16:3

Before you enter into any Battle, Contest, Game or War, consult with GOD, Pray and have an adequate "Game-Plan" in hand. **{For those times when you are thrust into instant action, say a Quick Prayer and flow in the Spirit** because according to 2 Timothy 4:2, we should "***be prepared in season and out of season***" of which we will expound upon more in the next section**.}** Assess your situation and those on your team to make sure that everyone is on the same page. For those that aren't Spiritually, Mentally or Physically ready for battle or competition, leave them behind {especially on Road-Trips.} When I was in sports, we used to traditionally post a scripture pertaining to "***Going to War" Deuteronomy 20: 1-8*** as the season begins in addition to the players refresh & re-read it prior to Road Trips in their private devotional time. *{For those of you that want your team in a more aggressive mindset have them read all of Chapter 20:1-20 and you won't have to give a Pre-game speech!}*

"When you go to war against your enemies and see horses and chariots and an army greater than yours, do not be afraid of them, because the Lord Your God, who brought you up out of Egypt, will be with you. When you are about to go into battle, the priest shall come forward and address the army. He shall say: "Hear, O Israel, today you are going into battle against your enemies. Do not be fainthearted or afraid; do not be terrified or give way to panic before them. For the Lord your God is the one who goes with you to fight for you against your enemies to give you victory. The officers shall say to the army: "Has anyone built a new house and not dedicated it? Let him go home, or he may die in battle and someone else may dedicate it. Has anyone planted a vineyard and not begun to enjoy it? Let him go home, or he may die in battle and someone else may enjoy it. Has anyone become pledged to a woman and not married her? Let him go home, or he may die in battle and someone else marry her." Then the officers shall add, ***"Is any man afraid or fainthearted? Let him go home so that his brothers will not become disheartened too." Deuteronomy 20: 1-8***

"Study to show thyself approved unto God, a workman who needeth not to be ashamed, rightly dividing the word of truth"-2 Timothy 2:15

To master the game, you must first become a student of the game.

To Win Consistently you should have knowledge of your Game and constantly be on top of you Game. **Life is a never ending *"learning experience"*** with new techniques, procedures and plays being developed every day. **Don't let anything distract you from gaining the knowledge you need to be successful.** *Never get complacent because you've experienced some symbolism of success.* **Stay focused and sharp because the day you lay off is the day it won't pay off.** You must become a student/scholar of the game before you Master it. **After you Master the Game, you then want to take Ownership.**

In the Sports world, we study film so that we can find our mistakes, correct our actions and then eliminate the mistakes. In both Sports & the Business and financial industry, we study and monitor stats, numbers & productivity to determine which areas are deficient, need attention or reduction, in addition to the areas that will bring abundant increase & profitability.

Sometimes in the game of life, you don't get that opportunity to roll back the film or the clock to correct your mistakes, so it's best to be on top of your game and minimize the possibility of mistakes before you leave the house, because it's a jungle out there.

"Self-Preservation is the First Law of Nature."

Even in the Sports World, one moment of indiscretion, loss of focus or lack of knowledge can adversely affect your career. This is why you study continuously in all facets of life to be aware of your atmosphere, surroundings and environment to be able to leave and return home safely everyday providing for your family, because sometimes even the hunters become the hunted when they stumble upon the wrong terrain or environment and find themselves no longer at the *"Top of the food Chain!"*

"When you are a Champion and at the top of your Game or on the Mountaintop, somebody is always painting a target on your back and trying to knock you off."

***Anticipate and avoid unnecessary conflicts in addition to never entering into a battle, contest or war where there is no reward.**

*__BE PREPARED__: *"Prior Preparation Prevents Poor Performance!"*

"Life is a Contact Sport. Protect yourself at all times in all facets of life."

"SELF-PRESERVATION IS THE FIRST LAW OF NATURE!"

"The most important thing to remember if you want to win a dog fight is to make sure that you bring the right dog"-Yusef L.Chew

When I was a member of the Boy Scouts coming up, they taught us to *"Always Be Prepared!"* I have adopted and adapted this motto to various segments of my Life. As part of my preparation process, I make every attempt to not only make sure that I am prepared but also those that will be working with me are up to speed as well to eliminate time wasting and to make sure that available personnel are utilized to their fullest extent to achieve Team-Goals.

As a Coach, leader, mentor, educator, exhorter or manager **it is very important to stay abreast of the moods, mindsets and tendencies of those on your team, inner circle or circumference**. It is your responsibility to **discover what is keeping your personnel from developing to their fullest potential** {on and off of the field of play.) **Encourage them to improve** in some area **every day**. **As a leader, it's not always what you know, but more so that of which you teach and**

how much is absorbed, attained and applied by those whom you lead.

"How can they know, except that they've been taught,"-Romans 10:15

"Preach the Word; ***be prepared in season and out of season****; correct, rebuke and encourage-with great patience and careful instruction"-2 Timothy 4:2*

Create a "Checks & Balance" System so that not only your Team/business is consistent, but everything that's related is double-checked for consistency, quality & clarity. This can help to eliminate problems and reduce challenges before they occur.). Know your personnel and keep in constant contact.

****Special Note:*** ***Always know what's going on in all aspects of your business, financial & personal life + the current trends in your industry. Regardless of the arena or entity, whether Military; Sports; Corporate America; Personal Relationships or Private Enterprise, you must "Game-Test" all applicants/prospects to show Position worthiness and Battle readiness. Prime example: In the military they have boot-camps; specialized training exercises, mock wars and battlefield simulation operations to gauge the quality of response, aptitude and performance. In sports they have combines, showcases; evaluation- training camps, Off-season Training Activities, scrimmages against each other and against***

simulated opponents to evaluate talent and potential to operate under stress, duress and game like situations. In the school system they have pop-quizzes & fire drills. In the public sector they have tornado drills/air-raid sirens. In the media they have news-flashes/public-service announcements. In the guise of building a team that you can compete with, you must "Game-Test" potential teammates to make sure that they are not "fly-by-night", "star-struck" or" fair-weather fans" and in it for the long-haul and not just for short-term benefits or entertainment purposes.

*****<u>Special Note:</u> In life when you are about to enter into competitive, tense or even hostile situations or environments, make sure that you are adequately prepared and have all protective measures, garments & equipment in place. In the Spiritual realm, the Bible states "to put on the full amour of God."***

******<u>Special Note:</u> Don't Expect What you don't Inspect! Game-Test to Bring out the Best!*** **Always *"Know" your personnel and keep in constant contact because People always act differently when they think you are watching them.***

***<u>COME CORRECT</u>**: *"Arrive with your Mind Right & YOUR GAME TIGHT!"*

"The Quickest Way to get defeated is to become distracted!"

"You have to always put yourself in position to Win."-Big-E aka Coach Eric Jones

"If you can't influence the outcome of a situation, then let it go. It's not for you to handle."-Marcellus Reed

Know what a Winner is & *"What it takes to Win"* before you begin! Understand How the System Works. Have a thorough understanding of any contest, event, situation or circumstance that you are contemplating getting involved in or with in addition to knowing the Rules, regulations, goals & aspirations of such including the anticipated rewards of coming out victorious or consequences & repercussions of failing to do so.

"Wisdom is the principal thing; therefore get wisdom and with all thy getting, get understanding"-Proverbs 4:7

"Many people take competition for granted, but competition breeds Champions!"-Norman Whitfield

"This is Not a Nice Game!"

What that means is that *somebody is going to "Win" and somebody is going to "Learn"*. Somebody is going to get their feelings hurt, egos crushed and dreams demolished. When you compete, it's not about being liked or loved, but being respected.

"Ain't no friends in Business or Battle!"

Which goes to say or imply is *that whenever someone opposes you, whether in Business, Life or on the court or playing field, one thing that they need to know is that you're going to try to take their head off so to speak or do your best to crush them in head to head competition."*

"Let all things be done decently and in order"-1 Corinthians 14:40

"Have some Class about yourself and always go First Class!"

If you're in a game and up by 40-50 points in the 4th Quarter by all means put the reserves in and let them get some experience and development, ***unless the opposition is a fierce rival or said /did something derogatory in the past in which case you have to teach them a lesson and run the score up*** **like a *"Las Vegas slot-machine"* and rub their nose in it like *a puppy dog that has pooped in the wrong place* to teach a lesson.**

When you travel, order uniforms, book hotels or make reservations for your group to eat, select Quality when at all possible, because your choices are a reflection of you and your brand or image and can be utilized as a *"Recruiting Tool"* if properly positioned. Plus, with the game being 90% mental, You want your team to travel well, look good, sleep good and eat good so that they can perform well or to the Best of their ability and have no excuses for a dereliction of duty. Always Give the Best that you have and expect the Best in return from Every Situation. When you set a "*Standard*" or a Level of Expectation it helps to increase productivity and eliminate "*Time-wasting*" because what's understood doesn't have to be discussed.

Special Note: ****Always Play by the Rules*** *{unless you make the Rules, and if so, don't always make them up as you go! Play Fair.* ***Cheaters never prosper! If you don't feel like you can win, then don't get in! You Beat 50% of the people by working hard! You Beat 40% more by doing what's Right! The last 10% is a dogfight! Laws, Rules & Regulations were put in place for a Reason to maintain order & reduce chaos! If they are to be broken, amended or up-ended please use the proper forum or avenues to bring about a peaceful change.***

***SEE YOURSELF WINNING**: "*Visualize on Winning the Prize*" & "*Never enter into a Contest where there are no spoils or Reward.*"

"Commit to the Lord whatever you do and He will establish Your Plans"-Proverbs 16:3

"When you have an Elephant sized Vision, you can't have mosquito faith!"-Big Ray

In order to win** or acquire the "Big-One***" you must first see yourself accomplishing this task. **You must have a mind to Prosper and a Will to Win.**

"Life is not made up of "the haves" and "the have-nots", but more so "the wills" and "the will-not."-Big Ray

The only reason men fail is due to broken focus. You must target that of which you desire the most and pursue it relentlessly.

To Win Consistently you should have knowledge of your Game and constantly be on top of you Game**.** **Life is a never ending *"learning experience"*** with new techniques, procedures and plays being developed every day**. Don't let anything distract you from gaining the knowledge you need to be successful.** *Never get complacent because you've experienced some symbolism of success.* **Stay focused and sharp because the day you lay off is the day it won't pay off.** You must become a student/scholar of the game before you Master it. **After you Master the Game, you then want to take Ownership.**

Whatever you want to become, whatever you want to achieve; whatever you want to have, accumulate or acquire they have a book on it. Find a book or books that can help to better your current conditions or situations. Read a few Chapters each night towards bettering yourself or your situation. "Study to show thyself approved." Readers are leaders and the reason why is because they are ahead of the game in reference to knowledge & application of that knowledge. The Bible says that the people shall perish for a lack of knowledge. Hosea 4:6. This passage holds true in various facets of life: Spiritual, Social, Physical, Financial, Business and Relationships.

Special Notes**: **There is a difference between reading and studying. Kind of like "entertainment & employment", there is going to be a difference in the level of focus and intensity including the willingness and ability to apply the information received.

"The only reason men fail is due to broken focus"

*****Special Note**: **Sometimes when operating in seemingly "losing situations" it may be easy to get weary, discouraged, lackadaisical or lack-luster in enthusiasm. A man once said;***

"The worst bankrupt in the world is a man who has lost his enthusiasm!"

Keep the faith, stay strong and stay committed to the task at hand. Sometimes it's not always about the score at the end of the game, but more so about the energy, effort and resources utilized to compete in the event. Sometimes you win by not quitting and finishing the task or event? Sometimes you win by improving performance and productivity from the

beginning to the end while simultaneously setting the tone for future endeavors. Sometimes you can win by dominating & annihilating your opponent, circumstances or situations. Other times, Reality sets in and you realize that you are proverbially "Beating a dead Horse" or "Riding a donkey in the Kentucky Derby" so to speak on your current project or placement and no matter how much effort you exhort it's not making a difference in productivity because the powers to be or associated with the project are unwilling or incapable of making a change for the better and you don't possess the authority to change or move them. This is when a Business decision has to be made. <u>Never set yourself up for failure</u>. When it becomes evident that you are "Riding a donkey in the Kentucky derby", it's time to change stables and /or running mates, because that's just a behind whipping waiting to happen. You don't have to go down with the ship (contrary to popular belief), especially if it isn't yours. There are plenty more where they came from.

"The same effort it takes to get to a row-boat or a dingy can be used to get to a yacht or a cruise ship"-Big Ray

<u>Special Note:</u> If you would just take the time to "Think" of 10-12 new things daily that you can do to improve your situation & implement them into your game plan over the***

next 21-40 days, watch & document the turnaround as your improvements transform into habits and later transitions into a Lifestyle.

THE GAME-PLAN: CREATE A DAILY SUCCESS ROUTINE AND HABITS FOR GREATNESS:

"You cannot change your Life until YOU CHANGE YOUR HABITS!"

"You are what you repeatedly do. Excellence therefore is not an act, but a habit"-Aristotle

"Sometimes in order to change your year, you have to change your atmosphere"-Big Ray

When you perform an act for 21-days straight it becomes a habit. When you continue with this new habit for 40 days or more, it now becomes a Lifestyle! (Google Search: "Winning is a Lifestyle")

"Success Habits"

****KEEP GOD FIRST, Because HE'S GOING TO BE FIRST* ANYWAY**!

"Seek ye first the kingdom of GOD and his righteousness and all these things shall be added unto you"-Mathew 6:33

If GOD isn't in it, don't accept the task/assignment or job regardless of how much it pays because it won't last long and the outcome could be more than you're willing to pay!

***Learn to Value Your Time! Time is a valuable commodity which once lost can never be regained!** The main difference between the poor and the wealthy is the value they put on their time. Don't waste it. Get a good concept of time and fully utilize it to that extent.*

Always take care of Home! Never get so caught up in the Business or outside world as to where you neglect or forget the real reason "Why" you are doing this in the first place. Home is where the heart is. If home isn't taken care of in all aspects, either you are doing too much or not enough! **In addition to taking care of home, make sure that you have adequate security mechanisms (including hidden cameras/microphones & motion detectors) in your home, business & office**. They now have the systems where you can check your home or business from the other side of the world via cell phone, tablet-PC or computer. Remember the root of Security is "Secure-it". A word to the wise should be sufficient! Also as you ascend the ladder of affluence make sure that you have an "armor bearer" on the team/speed-dial or someone that can double in that capacity until you develop a need to acquire personal or executive security. Ex-College football players serve well in this capacity.*

Not only are they educated and have the physique, but a team concept as well.

*"**Never discuss your problems with those incapable of helping you to come up with a solution!**"*

****Study to show thy self-approved!** To master your game, you must first become a student of the game. Whatever you want to become, whatever you want to achieve, accumulate or acquire they have a book on it. "Study to show thy self-approved." Readers are leaders and the reason why is because they are ahead of the game in reference to knowledge and application of that knowledge. The Bible says that the people shall perish for a lack of knowledge. This passage holds true in various facets of life: Spiritual, Social, Physical, Financial, Business and Relationships.*

****Always stay abreast of/ be aware of the competition and the position of the enemy. They are in business to put you out of Business (or take your head off!)***

****Turn Contacts into Contracts:** Make it a point to give away at least 5-10 business cards or flyers on a minimum daily which will result in coming into contact with 150-300 new people/contacts/prospects monthly & 1500-3000 new contacts a year of which a certain percentage will subscribe to your theory/product or service. With Success in Life being a Team-Effort and a Numbers Game, this "Success*

Habit" will help you to reach your goals sooner that just sitting back and waiting on them to come to you.

Campaign Like You're Trying to Make the Hall of Fame!* **"*If you put out 1000+ flyers a week, you will never go hungry"-Joan Louis. {When people hear your name, they need to know who you are and that you're "Good at what you do!"*

****Be detailed oriented**. It's the little things that count!*

**Don't be afraid to ask questions. They told us in football that the only dumb question is the un-asked question.*

****Don't Expect What you don't Inspect!** Game-Test to Bring out The Best!* Always check important items going out to customer's clients & prospects by having a second person double check the items prior to shipping or delivery. *(People always act differently when you are watching them. Create a "Checks & Balance" System so that not only your business but everything that goes out of the door is double-checked for consistency, quality & clarity. This can help to eliminate problems and reduce challenges before they occur.) Know your personnel and keep in constant contact. ***Always know what's going on in all aspects of your business, financial & personal life + the current trends in your industry**. Regardless of the arena or entity, whether Military; Sports; Corporate America; Personal*

Relationships or Private Enterprise, you must "Game-Test" all applicants/prospects to show Position worthiness and Battle readiness. Prime example: In the military they have specialized training exercises, mock wars and battlefield simulation operations to gauge the quality of response, aptitude and performance. In sports they have what they call scrimmages against each other and against simulated opponents to evaluate talent and potential to operate under stress, duress and game like situations. In the school system they have fire drills & pop quizzes. In the public sector they have tornado drills/air-raid sirens. In the media they have news-flashes/public-service announcements. In personal relationships, you must "Game-Test" potential mates to make sure that they are not "star-struck" or" fair-weather fans" and in it for the long-haul, not just for short-term benefits or entertainment purposes.

*** Don't make your Priorities a Minority!** *Get an Organizer, Desk Calendar or create a daily itinerary of things you intend to accomplish each day & check off completed items. Set alarm reminders on your phone calendars and memo sections as a back-up tool.*

Customize your environment to keep you motivated & inspired.

**Prepare for Your Destiny.*

Stay Clean & Keep Good Hygiene

**If you want to be Great, Surround Yourself with Greatness on a Regular Basis!*

****Be careful of the company you keep!*** *Sometimes people assume by association and image means a lot.*

**** Write a Book on whatever you're Good at and leave a legacy.*** *Don't let your history be a mystery. Remember "the game is to be sold, not to be told and when you sell it, make sure that you (and everybody associated) gets their cut/fair-share!" Not only does becoming an author put you in a select segment of society, it legitimizes your projects in addition to positioning you as an expert at what you do. You book can go places that you can't go in addition to opening doors that were previously inaccessible.*

***___Make Everyday Payday whether you're working or not.___ *Find out what Residual Income is. Also living paycheck-to-paycheck is alright as long as its daily paychecks!*

****Dress for Success!*** *Look The Part and Play The Part!*

****Always Put Yourself in Position for Recognition!***

"It's better to make the News that to be the News!"- Big Ray

When opportunities present themselves to establish your good name, integrity & reputation, seize the moment. A good name and reputation is more powerful than money. (Proverbs 22:1) Basically what we are saying is to provide things honest in the sight of all men and always be productive. This is not a statement to go out and toot your own horn (Proverbs 27:2) but more so to give people value for their money and never try to beat someone out of their money. Your gifts & talents will make a way before great men.

Learn to Eliminate Time Wasters and get rid of those that don't respect your time or your dime!

**Do Not Be Afraid to Walk Away from Mediocrity when it is an accepted practice and the majority present are unwilling to change*

***Treat Loyalty Like Royalty!** As my mother always said "Good Help is Hard to Find:"! When you find someone that's loyal to you and not just liking you for your paper or the things that you can do, take the time as often as possible to reward and let that person know that they are very much appreciated. You will definitely find out who your true friends are when you lose the limelight or things get tight! It's always good to have Good People on Your Team! You never know when you are going to need them to make a play?*

***Remember that Business & Personal Business don't always mix!** Unless you're married or closely related or If it's not a family owned business, keep* *your business and your family totally separated until it's time to bring an offspring up and teach them how to take over the business. Only those closest to you can hurt you and it's often harder to retaliate or take legal action against a relative because you might be the same one having to bail them out or pay their hospital bill!*

**Get an intro-song/theme song or a gospel hit that makes you feel Great and play it anytime you don't feel on top of your game!*

**Learn how to play Golf. A lot of deals and quality contacts are made on the Golf-course. A hidden attraction is that this is a game is that requires participants to be honest, possess integrity and have Self-discipline because of the lack of a referee. Imagine how many relationships and financial transactions would have lasted longer and been stronger had the parties involved possessed the aforementioned qualities?*

**Walk at least 1-3 miles daily & Brainstorm during these walking sessions.*

**Always carry a mini-digital recorder with you at all times to take notes on any ideas you may come up with while they are fresh on your mind.*

** Go where the $ goes and go where the $ flows & grows!* ***People usually spend their money in 7-main areas: Church, Food, Hair, Clothing; Automobiles; Entertainment & Housing! You should have your hand, your ear and your***

marketing message in at least 4 or 5 out of the 7? *It is a given that a majority of people are always going to Praise GOD, need something to eat, need a haircut or style; need something to wear, someplace to stay & Transportation.*

**Don't be afraid to ask for "Quality" referrals from family members, friends, customers & clients. Remember that a closed mouth rarely gets fed!*

****Train the people that you delegate tasks to do the things the way you like them done.*** *Hire for attitude & train for aptitude! As a business owner or leader you are always constantly evaluating the people who help to achieve team goals. If you have people on your team who aren't willing to work to improve the team, help the team reach its goals or to bring in new business, you should evaluate why they are still with your team or business?*

**Get a competent mentor who is successful in your field.*

**Don't waste your vote.*

****Protect Your Name! It is going to outlast you!***

**When contemplating entering into new interpersonal relationships have a pad with at least 25+ or more qualities listed that you are looking for in a mate then grade out/pre-screen new applicants on a percentage basis of how they stack up against your list to eliminate wasting your time, their time or your dime! (If you didn't have at least 20-25* *preferred qualities listed, you didn't give it much considerable thought & go back and think thoroughly. They should grade out at 70% or more to be your friend; 80% or more to be a girlfriend/boyfriend & 90% or better for marriage material.) Nobody is perfect, but there is someone perfect for you! This eliminates having to go through 9 or 10 candidates just to find out number 4 was the right one!*

**Develop your craft and become a Specialist, a Technician or a Master at what you do!*

***Remember: The Golden Rule!** In elementary or pre-school you were lead to believe that the Golden Rule meant to do unto others as you would have to do unto you in order to create a cooperative atmosphere of peace, order, tranquility and non-violence toward others. Fast-forward years later to post-adolescence; where you start experiencing the "Real-World" that is "Cold, Cruel & Cut-throat" with chaos and not so nice actions going on which brings out the true revelation of the meaning of this term. {Treat others like they need to be treated according to their actions & productivity and to remember that he who has the gold, rules.*

**Go Where You are Celebrated & not where you are tolerated!*

PAY YOUR TAXES! A guy named "Uncle-Sam" (who is probably not related to you) has to get his cut of whatever it is that you may be making even* *though he didn't help you to earn it. As bad as it may sound, it can get worse because if he doesn't get his cut and he finds out, he will send his 3-letter cousins "the alphabet-boys" to come collect it for him and it won't be nice! Consider taxes as one of your costs of doing business and pay them up front on a quarterly basis so that you don't have to come up with a lump sum at the end/beginning of the year.*

** Follow a Plan and not a man (nor a woman.)*

**Become a Lifetime Enjoyment Specialist!*

*****Keep at least 10 millionaires on speed-dial in your phone:*** They have connections and access to people, products & services that other people can only dream about. Remember *"Team-work makes the Dream Work"!* One of the Best Motivating Factors that you can have in Business is Financial Backing! Also keep in mind that a lot of people with resources are always looking for good opportunities to multiply their reserves, gifts & talents with minimal effort. *VERY IMPORTANT: Always Use WISDOM and Make sure that before you approach someone asking to utilize their hard earned $ & that you have thoroughly researched and game-tested your idea or proposal to make sure that its Full-proof, Legitimate & Reputable (and not just operate off of hearsay & rhetoric or from what "they say!" One of the quickest ways to turn a Friend into a Foe and ruin your Reputation is to play with their $ like its "Monopoly-$!" Avoid approaching them with "Get Rich Quick*

Schemes" or the "You have to Rush and get on board now because it's a Ground-Floor Opportunity." Position yourself so that whenever they hear from you, they are eager to hear what you have to offer/say because they believe that you are bringing value or something that can enhance joy, peace & happiness in their life or inner circle.

** **If you going to hang around "broke-people" make sure that they possess one or more of the following:** A mind to prosper; A unique talent or skills; Information or contacts.*

**In the guise of Relationships you can be in one of 6-positions: The One; One-Gone, The Next One, The Last One; Not the One & The Only One. Choose Wisely!*

****Refuse to drive or operate a vehicle that is not insured except in cases of Extreme Emergency/Life or Death Situations!** It is better to walk, catch a cab or ride with a friend/ neighbor than to operate a vehicle without insurance and have a mishap occur.*

****Never let someone that is irresponsible or incapable of coming up with the insurance deductible drive or operate your vehicle!***

**Never loan your vehicle to someone non-related unless it's for business purposes or they are working for you in a business capacity!*

Always do visual inspections of a vehicle before you operate it, especially the tires, fuel & pressure gauges! The Life You Save could be Your Own!

Always Play by the Rules! Cheaters never prosper! If you don't feel like you can win, then don't get in! You Beat 50% of the people by working hard! You Beat 40% more by doing what's Right! The last 10% is a dogfight! Laws, Rules & Regulations were put in place for a Reason to maintain order and reduce chaos! If they are to be broken, amended or up-ended please use the proper forum or avenues to bring about a peaceful change.

If you ever have a legal issue or have to deal with the law; keep your mouth shut and consult with an attorney or a legal-aid society before speaking words that could be used against you in a court of law!

**Don't Quit Your Day Job until your secondary source or side-hustle is bringing in 3x-4x that of your regular salary. Sometimes people get caught up on "Hype-Speeches" & "Get-Rich Quick" schemes and forget to wait until the vision manifests before giving up their primary source of income. Use Wisdom!*

"When GOD gives you a Vision, he will make Provision!"-George Foster

"When a man gives you a vision, you need to set a deadline of when it will manifest because a goal or a vision without a deadline is just a wish or a dream!"

**When you find an "excuse" don't pick it up!*

**Know your strengths and weaknesses. Major in your strengths and manage your weaknesses.*

**Specialize in your specialty!*

***Eliminate anyone or anything that causes you to be ineffective. Eliminate anyone or anything that breaks your focus.**

**When you show up, a difference should be made!*

* ***Describe how you will solve problems, provide value and reward for your prospective clients & team members (because you will receive no reward until you do so. $ is a reward you receive when you solve problems for others.)***

**Don't put Million Dollar ideas into dollar notebooks. Get a leather-bound notebook or a Tablet PC.*

***Whenever you see something that makes you smile, buy it and put it in front of you!**

***Always check your own parachute and double-check your clip to make sure that you have "real" bullets in it!**

**"When things go wrong don't go with them!"-Les Brown*

**Make your assets pay your liabilities!*

**Don't expect other people to operate off of the level of knowledge that you have attained!*

***"Never interrupt an enemy when he is making a mistake"-Napoleon Bonaparte**

Chapter 49
THE GAME IS TO BE SOLD, NOT TOLD!

**This Chapter is intended to help you keep things in "Proper Perspective."*

The "*Game*" refers to whatever your "*Livelihood*", "*Specialty*", "*Gift*" or area of Expertise is. This Chapter is specifically intended for Professionals and those in Business or Business Ownership, because **most people go into Business to Make Money** and **Professionals "*GET PAID*" Consistently!** *Amateurs DON'T*! Amateurs, this chapter may not be for you {until you're ready to Change Your Status} even though "Everybody Plays an Important Part in the Ecosystem." The Only thing "*FREE*" in this world is "*AIR*" & "*OPPORTUNITY*" *{because they are selling water by the bottle and oxygen by the tank.* On the back of your dollar, it states ***"IN GOD WE TRUST" in Bold Letters.*** When you get to reading and interpreting some of the foreign language on the back of that same dollar, you will come to find out that "***All others must pay!***"

"It is better to trust in the Lord than to put confidence in man."-Proverbs 118:8

Have you ever stopped to ask yourself "***Why does the currency in a country whose primary language is English have inscriptions & decryptions on it in languages that are mainly un-interpretable with common knowledge by the majority of its users or inhabitants?***" The system is designed to lead you astray and for the

"*Rich to get Richer*" and the Poor to be just that. Unless you educate yourself and get knowledge on the purpose and processes of money being a medium of exchange, a lot of times, it will pass you by. The Bible says that *"my people perish for a lack of knowledge…"-Hosea 4:6 {some translations state "are destroyed" instead of "perish."*

If you're in Business or a Professional, there is nothing wrong with annual or semi-annual giveaways, having loss-leaders or giving away samples, promotional items or "*Test-Drives*" to attract and bring in "*New-Business*" nor having "*Referral based incentives*" to reward, motivate and inspire your current clientele or workforce, but ***you can't give away the whole business***. **People don't Respect "*FREE*"** unless it's "*Gift Wrapped*" or in a "*Sponsorship*" package. The only time "*telling your business*" is acceptable is when its work related in the guise of advertising, marketing or prospecting for new business and clients or offering the opportunity to become a part of your business for expansion & growth purposes. The Bible makes reference to "*All hard work leads to profit, but mere talk only leads to poverty"-Proverbs 14:23* & *"Do not muzzle the ox when he treadeth the corn and the servant is worthy of his hire"- 1Timothy 5:19*

In the **Sports realm**, if you're at a place where they're not "*buying in*" to your programs, theories, systems or analogies; don't give it away for free. Just because it's not valued in a particular market or region, doesn't mean that your information is not Valuable. "One man's trash is another man's Treasure." Sometimes you have to take your show on the road and "***Go where you're celebrated and not where you're tolerated***!" The Bible makes reference to *"A prophet is not without honor except in his own town and his own home" Mark 13:57; Mark 6:4; Luke 4:24*

Even in the guise of the **Educational Process** which includes ***"Acquired"* knowledge & *"Bought"* knowledge**. Acquired knowledge is usually obtained through experiences, situations and circumstances. Bought knowledge is usually acquired through privileged information, higher or specialized education processes, seminars or workshops & literature. In the common vernacular, you may hear references to **being *"taught"* & *"schooled?"*** Translation- When you have been "*taught*', it was because you were educated or trained in reference to a certain topic or subject matter. When you hear the terminology about being "*schooled*", this refers to learning a lesson from experience or sometimes from having been fooled in some area or another due to lack of knowledge.

A lot of times people don't learn to appreciate "*Education*" or start to take it seriously until it costs them something, they have to pay for it or they are *forced to "Learn" due to situations and circumstances*. A prime example of this is Public School, Private School and College Education. A lot of people take the Public School Education for granted because it's a Right and everyone is entitled. Now, when you transition over to Private School Education, you have qualifying criteria for acceptance and the "*Privilege*" of attending and for the most part, it's going to cost you something unless you're a "*special case*" and you're doing a trade off for "*goods & services*". Now when you get to the College Level, almost everyone has to pay unless you're on Scholarship and bringing something to the table other than a "*derriere and a smile.*"

The main Reason You Go to College is to "*Learn How to Make Money*" or become "Professional" or "Certified" to make Money. What they don't tell you is that you don't have to wait until you graduate to start making money. Even in an "*Amateur*" or "*Novice*" status, there are ways to **make your learning process or experience "*Profitable*", "*Rewarding*" and Mutually Beneficial.** Keep in mind the words "***Supply & Demand***" and that the way you make money is by displaying your "*gifts*", finding your "***niche***" and **solving problems for others**. *{Read Proverbs 18:16 & Ecclesiastes10:19*

Another scenario in the Educational Process is that **Education is a Business** and *according to the level of your education, where you were educated and by whom you were instructed will have a direct bearing* *on how you are viewed, received and rewarded by society*. A lot of people don't understand the "perceived Value" of an Education and have a hard time or are averse to paying for the "Power" that the information, associations & connections that education provides. Ask yourself what is the price of getting educated at **Hampton, Harvard, Howard or Stanford** *versus the variance in costs and prestige from getting educated at your local community college or State school?* Life is about Choices. **Choose Not to Lose!** In Life, you will make some Good Decisions and some not so good decisions of which there may be consequences and repercussions.

"Study to show thyself approved unto God, a workman who needeth not to be ashamed, rightly dividing the word of truth"-2 Timothy 2:15

"The instructions that you follow, will determine the future that you create"-Mike Murdock

In **Corporate America**, they will dangle that apple, carrot; trinket or dollar in your face to **sell you the "*Dream*" of Living Life Happily Ever after** to keep you motivated and inspired to make them as much money as possible. What they don't tell you is that if you utilized 20-30% of the effort with the "*same enthusiasm*" that you exhibited in the corporate sector into your own business, you could bring in the same amount or more working your own business and developing your own Empire. The sad part about this is scenario is most people "can't handle the truth" or don't want to face these facts until after they have invested 10-20 years of their lives into the dream of corporate America and have exhausted a large portion of their "youthful exuberance" or energy needed to kick off a business of their own. When you go into corporate America, you have to **go in with a "*Game plan*"** whether it is a 3yr, 5yr or 10yr plan to get in, stack your "paper", learn the systems and make valuable connections **to be utilized in future endeavors.** Do not get comfortable or complacent because they can and sometimes will pull the carpet out from under your feet and you have to be prepared to land correctly when this situation arises.

In Relationships, realize that **GOD *sends people into your life for a Reason, a Season or a Lifetime*.** "***People will come and go.***" It is up to you to **realize as to what "*intent*" that people have come into your life for and fully utilize them to that extent**. Some people will tell you that it's not right to use people? I'm going to tell you that people are a resource to be utilized to achieve your goals and aspirations, but it's not alright to "*misuse*" people. Always be fair in your business dealings and personal relationships. Realize that **relationships are a process of exchange and sometimes dissolve when they are no longer mutually beneficial** or the exchange dissipates. A lot of times people forget that whatever it takes to acquire or engage in a certain situation or entity is also sometimes necessary to remain in place to maintain that same situation or entity. Change is inevitable. Sometimes you embrace change and other times, change is instituted upon you. Things change and people change. ***"Dating"* consists of gather data to see if you want continue to journey farther in the same direction with a person or entity** or change pathways. **When or if that time ever comes to part ways have or create an *"Exit strategy* "**and make every attempt to do so peacefully and amicably. Life is about "*Choices*", **Choose Not to Lose!** If they're not for you, "*clean & clear your plate or slate*" & "*get rid of excess baggage*" so you can have room for the "*Chosen-1*" that is supposed to be there. **Time is a Valuable Commodity which once lost can never be regained**. **Never spend "Major Time" with minor people** unless they are "*paying like I'm weighing*" for your goods, products or services.

Be cognizant of the fact that every situation is not for you and if it's not on the path between you and your goals, it's not for you to deal with and May often times be a distraction.

Don't be quick to jump into "*New Relationships*" too fast without giving it considerable thought. *A lot of times the first 60-90 days of a "New Relationship" are all a front or a façade and most of the time, you're just dealing with their "Representative."* Use patience and wisdom to save yourself a lot of headaches, time and trouble.

"Before You come out of Your Pocket and Spend a "dime", You had better strategize and use your mind"-Big Ray

Learn to eliminate "*Time-Wasters*" and get yourself a "***SYSTEM***" {*which stands for "**Save Yourself Time, Energy & Money**"*} to **eliminate, block & lock *"Time-Wasters"*, *"Fools"* and *those who don't Respect Your Time or your dime* from your schedule.**

Special Note: *Everything is not always a "hustle" or about a dollar, even though it's amazing that even in the amateur arena, they want you "hustling & humping" at a fast pace for free. Don't be afraid to donate and give back to them that have helped you to come up along the way or from where you have received, especially to the communities in which you live to help make society a better place in addition to helping today's youth develop on a positive path so that you don't have to deal with them in adverse situations later in life.*

****Special Note:*** *Organize your schedule to eliminate "Time-wasters" & "Distractions." The time wasted with fools can be invested with Winners!*

****** The Breakdown:***

Imagine that you have your own personal Kingdom and Sanctuary available to you fully equipped with all of the items and ambience to keep you "Happy" & "Satisfied." Now Picture yourself as a "King" or "Queen" of this Wonderful Kingdom & Sanctuary and think of some creative means to describe you "Kingdom & Sanctuary" in addition to whom you would allow access and why? To begin with, let's start off with the names. Since we don't do "magic", we will call it "Miracle" Kingdom; and due to the fact that "Magic Kingdom" is owned by "Disney World", we won't call it "Disney's World"; we will call it "Your World". As for whom you would allow "Full" or "Direct" access, it would more than likely be those who are in your "Inner-circle" or on "Your Team". Now close your eyes and visualize on this "Miracle Kingdom" in "Your World" for a minute or two before I come back to you with some "News that you can use" plus information and concepts to enlighten your experience.

Knowledge is the new **"currency"** ***and access to Information equates to*** **"Power."** *Sometimes access to information on* "the Game" *can be bigger than* "the Game" *itself, because playing* "the Game" *or being a* "Player" *in* "the Game" *can sometimes have an* "Expiration" *date. When you take ownership or have dominion over information on* "the Game", *now you can position yourself to profit and prosper from it for a Lifetime and for* *generations to come after you're gone. Ask Walt Disney and Al Davis.*

Now back to the Kingdom at hand: **"Miracle Kingdom"** ***in*** **"Your World."** *If you spent time, energy, efforts and resources to develop and build an Empire The "Miracle Kingdom" in "Your World", why would you take and give the "Blue-Prints" + Recipes for Success in your* "Miracle Kingdom" *or"* **Power"** *over* "Your World" *to someone non-associated or not on your Team without being compensated?* **If you owned "Disney World" or "McDonald's" would you give it away for free or Charge admission and Franchise it out?** *If you give it away for free, how long do you think it will last and where do you think you would end up?*

FOOD FOR THOUGHT!

- **Bouncing Back from a Setback**

In this game we call "Life", sometimes you will "*Win*" and other times you will "*Learn*" that in every competition, situation or circumstance that you enter into or deal with, there is a distinct possibility that you can and sometimes will come up on the "*Learning*" side, and when this occurs, make sure that you don't have to "*Learn*" the same "*Lesson*" twice.

"A mistake committed more than once is a Decision."

As we tell people that are associated with us on a regular basis "Choose not to Lose!" It doesn't matter whether you're operating as an individual or as part of a group; team or organization, the method or strategy that you employ or utilize to come back or *"Bounce back"* from a setback will set the stage for future endeavors. Keep in mind that *"all eyes are on you"* and that you're constantly under surveillance & scrutiny, so use wisdom & intelligence and choose *"Wisely"* when setting your game-plan for Success. Don't always try to comeback or bounce back from a setback operating off of emotions, become sometimes our emotions can lead us astray. Whenever you get into *"Bounce back or Come-back Mode"*, it is very important that you don't let your ego or attitude or enthusiasm override *"common-sense"* {which isn't so common anymore) or good judgment.

"Never make a Long-Term Decision based upon a Short-Term Situation."

As we mentioned in another chapter, *"If in doubt, Call a Time-Out" or if* you need to disappear for a *"minute"* at *"half-time"* to regroup and get your head together, then by all means do so. Other times, if your setback involved a season and the season is over, sometimes you may want to go off into the *"Wilderness" for 21-40 days to "Get closer to GOD and flow in the Spirit to renew your Strength, Get Direction & Correction"{Read Romans 8:11}* to polish up your game and comeback in "***Beast-mode" or "Clint Eastwood mode."***

Another reason that we mentioned going off in the "*Wilderness" for 21-40 days is to develop new "Habits"* and a "*Lifestyle conducive to Winning"* in addition to the fact that in the game of Life, sometimes it's a Jungle out there and "*You may need to get away from or eliminate distractions so that you can "Study to show yourself approved" and focus on "WHY"* you are in this position; "*WHAT'S"* your purpose for being here and what's important to you?

"A double minded man is unstable in all his ways" - James 1:8

In the Sports world, we study film so that we can find our mistakes, correct our actions and then eliminate the mistakes. In both Sports and the Business and financial industry, we study and monitor stats, numbers & productivity to determine which areas are deficient, need attention or reduction, in addition to the areas that will bring abundant increase & profitability.

Sometimes in the game of life, you don't get that opportunity to roll back the film or the clock to correct your mistakes, so it's best to be on top of your game and minimize the possibility of mistakes before you leave the house, because it's a jungle out there. Everybody in the jungle has an agenda, a job, objective or a purpose when they wake up.

When the Deer, the Antelope & the Wilder beast wake up every day and leave the house, their objective is not to get eaten alive and return home safely. When the Lions, Tigers, Jaguars & Leopards leave the house every day, their objective is to obtain something to eat and bring it back home to feed their family. Until you can develop your game or position yourself to where you are no longer the hunted, you have to take precautionary measures to survive in this game called *"Life."*

"Self-Preservation is the First Law of Nature."

Even in the Sports World, one moment of indiscretion, loss of focus or lack of knowledge can adversely affect your career. This is why you study continuously in all facets of life to be aware of your atmosphere, surroundings & environment to be able to leave & return home safely everyday providing for your family, because sometimes even the hunters become the hunted when they stumble upon the wrong terrain or environment and find themselves no longer at the *"Top of the food Chain!"*

"When you are a Champion and at the top of your Game or on the Mountaintop, somebody is always painting a target on your back and trying to knock you off."

"We are what we repeatedly do. Excellence therefore is not an act, but a HABIT!" -Aristotle

"80% of your success is going to be achieved by you showing up and being busy." -Armani Valentino

"90% or most businesses failed because they quit or they don't have a Marketing Plan." –Armani Valentino

"People do not decide to become extraordinary. They decide to accomplish extraordinary things." – Edmund Hillary

The first thing you need to do before you go into *"Bounce back Mode or Comeback Mode"* is to make a decision or a "Goal" to just that and devise a plan.

The Next Step after you figure out your purpose, mission or that which you are working to achieve, acquire or encompass is to develop a Plan of action or a *"Road-map"* of how to get to the place called *"There."*

A Goal is the place where you want to be. A Plan is a *"Road-map"* of how to get there; a *"Blueprint"* of how to put it together when you arrive and a *"Recipe"* of all of the ingredients, processes and tools necessary to bring it to fruition or manifest.

Once you have a plan in hand, put your *"Game-face"* on, *"**Adjust your Attitude**"* and ***"Get Your Mind Right"*** because it's ***"GAME-TIME"!*** Not only do you need to have a *"**Positive Mental Attitude**";* you need to have a ***"Go Get it Attitude."***

"When you go out to compete, you have to compete like you are running in the Kentucky derby!"-Bishop Don "Magic" Juan

You have to transform your mindset to encompass the tasks at hand or associated with creating a Dynasty, financial empire or portfolio. Similar to that of a "*Prime Athlete*" as he prepares to compete, you have to put your "*game-face*" on and have your mind, body and soul conditioned to go "*a full 4-Quarters*" and several overtimes if necessary in order to fulfill or achieve your goals. You have to be "*Relentless*" like a boxer in a Prize fight where the only way you lose is if you quit fighting or allow your opponents to outwork you and get knocked out. Once you step in to your arena or area of expertise, you need to be focused and **check all "*distractions*" and "*unnecessary baggage*" or "*dead-weight*" prior to leaving the house or in the parking lot; because 1-mistake could cost you your opportunity or set you back to ground zero.**

"The Quickest Way to get defeated is to Lose Focus."

Whatever your venture, product or service, your job is to make it "*Grow, Go & Get some More!*" With Prior Preparation Preventing Poor Performance, you need to be at least 3-steps ahead of the game and be prepared to adapt and adjust to certain shifts or changes in momentum during those times when Life throws you a curve to still obtain optimal results and give yourself a cushion to absorb or deflect any unforeseen blows, hits or accidents. There will be times in Life where you may not achieve every goal within the allotted period of time or reach the finish line before every competitor. Sometimes, you don't always win by crossing the finish line first, but more so by crossing the finish line. This is what may be referred to as a *"Pass/Fail"* option which is determined solely on the participation and productivity of the participant.

"It's not always how you start, but how you finis*h"- *Devin Wyman

When you start an assignment, task or enter into a competition, compete and complete the assignment or task as if you were working for **GOD,** your family or a special cause where *"loosing is not an option".* Prepare your mind, body and soul to complete your task regardless of circumstances and not get weary in well doing. If you are in business, finish what you start and get a polished/ finished product to the people and communicate with your client base in the event of temporary setbacks. If you're competing in the sports arena, always compete and perform to the best of your ability as to win the prize regardless of the activity of those around you or lackluster performances by teammates. If your arena is entertainment, the show must go on and *"1-monkey doesn't stop the show."* If you are an entrepreneur, have a product, service or manufacturing don't give up or quit in the face of adversity, because you'll win if you don't quit. When situations arise and it appears that you may have to call a proverbial *"time-out"*, complete and fulfill all current/present orders and put future orders on hold unless fulfilling current orders would present a health risk.

When you experience a nice payday, *"hit a lick"* or have a successful venture, don't go and blow all of the profits. Restock, *"Re-up"* or reinvest a certain percentage of the profits back into the business to make sure that you have operating capital and materials to function in the future during tight turbulent times or when things get slow in the financial arena or due to seasonal demands. If your business or venture deals with non-perishable goods, get about 3-weeks -3-months of goods and supplies stocked up in advance. If your business or venture deals with perishable goods, then you should have at least 3-days of advance stock on hand in addition to 5-10 additional supplier resources in case your primary source dries up or experiences adversity and is unable to deliver. Just because 1 source or entity stops producing, doesn't mean that you have to stop producing, because "***Winning is a Lifestyle.***"

When you go into *"Bounce back-Mode"* with your own products & services, make sure that you get focused on the task at hand and be cognizant of the various differences of markets and the customer base that you will be serving, in addition to making sure that you are organized before you leave the House. Same thing goes for your team if you have one.

"3-Things will get you beat in this "Game", Being Un-Organized, Un-Disciplined & Un-Conditioned!"

"The Quickest Way to get defeated is to Lose Focus."

Other Factors that will contribute to your Success in *"Bounce back-Mode"* are:

- Your Mood & Attitude as well as your approach.
- Food, Nutrition and Proper Rest prior to event
- Exercise, Fitness Level and proper Conditioning.
- A fertile market or environment with qualified prospects that have a willingness and ability to purchase or subscribe to your products, goods or services.
- Prior Preparation and Proper Promotion.
- Appearance, Attire, Grooming and Mode of Transportation, because sometimes it's not always about getting from Point "A" to Point-"B", but more so of how you arrive.
- Whether or not your Product /Service helps to Make $, Save $, Time, Energy or Efforts.

Special Note: ***Attitude, Approach and Location play a very important part in your success when going into "Bounce back-Mode". The same effort that it takes to make "dimes or a few dollars" in one market can be utilized to make "Millions" in another market that's ripe, fertile and receptive to your products/ services, concepts or ideas. With the "Right Research" & Prior Preparation, you can come up "Exponentially" in a market that's***

"starving" or "thirsty" for your concepts & ideas. By utilizing the concepts of the Laws & Rules of "Supply & Demand" in a proper fashion, your product/services can become a "Household" name. A prime example of this is one of my good friends that was famous in the clothing industry who used to make $2k-5k daily and $7k-12k a day on the weekends vending & selling T-shirts, hats & concession items after an NBA-Team won "Back-to-Back" Championships. Way back in the day, when the author was new to the game and in college, I tapped into this concept (with only $60 in my pocket) and made $2,300 {actually it was more like $2,700 but I had spent $400 on Entertainment, Travel & Expenses + Restocking} in an 18-hour period working for someone else on a road trip making only $2-5 commission per item. Imagine what happened when I had branched out and went independent? Now you see why the college days are supposed to be some of the Best days of your Life. My theory is that it doesn't have to stop there, (because Life is an ever learning experience) if you remember the concepts and continually discover new markets and territories. New Champions are being made in various entities and markets Year Round. All you have to do is "Believe to Receive" and tap into the "Source" & "Supply a Need."

Chapter 50
UNLEASH THE BEAST WITHIN:

In the sports world & the entertainment industry, a "***Beast***" is described as someone or some entity that is dominant in their industry and on top of their game. In the animal kingdom there are various animals which fall under the category of carnivorous {which are meat eaters}. In order to be a "meat-eater", you have to be a natural hunter and sometimes this will require you to be aggressive, assertive, intelligent, and strategic plus a go-getter. In a biblical analogy, it states that

"From the days of John the Baptist until now The Kingdom of Heaven suffereth violence and the violent take it by force." - Mathew 11:12

(Please keep this in proper perspective and realize that the word "*violent*" means aggressive action, not necessarily a harmful act against another.) In the guise of obtaining your goal, sometimes you want to be a force to be reckoned with and at other times you want to be in "stealth" mode and fly under the radar so to speak. As there are various methods to hunt from primitive to next generation, we will describe various attributes of different species in the animal kingdom to tap into for illustration purposes. Some of these will include: **The Lion, Eagle, Guerilla, Shark, and Horse** {not a carnivore. All of these have some similarities as well as vast differences that we want you to tap into and adapt to some of your business principles.

We like ***the Lion** because it represents strength and is known as the King of the Jungle. Lions usually hunt in a pack which requires team-work and they normally have a lot of structure and order in their pride team or family of lions. Just like the lion, we want you to be the King of Your Craft & get treated like the Royalty that you are! Also, we want you to be able to work in a team-like setting and align yourself with like-minded individuals to achieve your team-goals. *Another good thing about the Lion is that it never loses sleep over the opinions of sheep.*

*Like **the Eagle** who soars in high places that a lot of other birds can't reach, we want you to soar to higher heights in your endeavors that other people deem unfathomable. Out of all of the birds the Eagle is considered to be the smartest & strongest in addition to being able to fly the highest. The Eagle is highly respected and known for pretty much traveling alone or in pairs and still obtains optimal results in the animal kingdom Like Navy-SEALS . Sometimes coming up in the Game of Life, you will need to make things happen for yourself, be highly effective obtaining optimal results with little or no help until you can develop your business to the point to where it attracts the kind of people you need on your team to assist. In retrospect, you don't always need a team of people to be successful at what you do; you just need to tap into the Champion within to Succeed. In the sports world, a lot of coaches use the phrase "There is no "I" in TEAM." Our response to this is that there is one in Champion and two in Championship. On the Professional Sports Level (as is also sometimes true in business), "when competition begins, friendship ends". {Perspective point: You always want to have good sportsmanship, play fair and abide by the rules of the game. You have to have character, integrity and principals in whatever arena that you deal in. You never want to develop a reputation of one that plays dirty or uses unfair business practices as this could prove detrimental to long-term business success). One guy used to tell me back when I were in the "hair-industry" that "it ain't no friends in business". Learn to separate Personal from Business. In corporate America we were taught that being a team player comes about after one completes their own assignments. The main gist of this is that you at times have to be able to operate independently of others and still obtain optimal RESULTS! Say to yourself; "If it's to be, It's Up to Me!" Sometimes in Life you have to be a "1-Man (or Woman) Army or Wrecking Crew. A good thing about being an Eagle is that whenever you find yourself in the midst of confusion, chickens, ducks, pigeons or any other animal that eats off of the ground, you can flap your wings a few times and orbit into an atmosphere that smells sweet and is clear.

***The Guerilla** is known for its strength and its magnificent fur. In our world, the guerilla has a duel meaning and is very special. Google or search the term "*Guerilla Marketing*" and what it entails and you are about to encompass another world when it comes to obtaining your goals with limited resources and still come out like the *King-Kong* of your industry. As Denzel Washington's character in the movie training day stated *"King-Kong ain't got nothing on me!"*

*The reason we mentioned **"The Shark"** is because of its ability to operate swiftly in stealth mode under water and still dominate in its environment. When you enter the water as a human being, you are no longer at the top of the "*food-chain*" {especially the farther you get from shore.} When you enter the water of doing business during turbulent times, we want you to be the Hunter and not the hunted, to survive and not get eaten alive. You have to be able to adapt and adjust to any situation or terrain and overcome obstacles to remain victorious!

*The reason we added **the Horse** {even though it's not a carnivore) is because of its size, strength, endurance and ability to go long distances. Another attribute that we like about the Horse is that even though it's not a natural hunter, in the animal kingdom, the horse is not one of the "most-hunted" because of its strength, size, speed and ability to defend itself and fight back with velocity, intensity and power. One blow or kick from a Horse can paralyze or break bones in an adversary. Some of the attributes from the horse that we want you to adapt and to obtain are the ability to go long distances and finish the tasks at hand. Also, even though you may not always be in hunt mode, we want you to ***position yourself as to where predators know that you are not to be hunted or tampered with due to potential consequences and repercussions.***

+In order to be successful, you are going to have to be able to adapt & apply certain attributes of each of the aforementioned animals/Beasts to your game plan at various points along your journey to survive and achieve Greatness!

"The most important thing to remember if you want to win a dog fight is to make sure that you bring the right dog"-Yusef L.Chew

Plug into a Proven Success System

Plug into a Proven Success System and duplicate your efforts. **SYSTEM stands for** ***Save Your Self Time, Energy & Money!

Sometimes you don't need to be a "Rocket-Scientist"; sometimes you just need a Rocket!

"You don't always have to reinvent the wheel; just paint a new stripe on it with your name on the side!"-Big Ray

Vogue Tire company did this by painting an extra/yellow stripe on a tire, "*nick-named mustard & mayonnaise*" and makes a killing selling these tires to people who wanted to be different, outstanding or proverbially doing more than the next guy? No knock against the company because their product looks Great and motivates/stimulates the mind of those who purchase them which makes them a worthwhile purchase because ***sometimes in life you have to do what it takes to "jump-start" your enthusiasm regardless of what other people think*** .

-You have to find your "niche."

GET UP OFF OF YOUR BEHIND & DO SOMETHING ABOUT IT!

"All Hard Work Leads to Profit, but mere talk only leads to Poverty."-Proverbs 14:23

"You will always remain the same until the pain of remaining the same becomes too great."

"You are what you repeatedly do. Excellence therefore is not an act, but a habit"-Aristotle

The only thing standing in the way of YOUR SUCCESS is Atmosphere & Your Fear! Create or Find a System *Save Yourself Time, Energy, Money* , Product or Service and Duplicate Your Efforts! "Prior Preparation Prevents Poor Performance: **If your destination is Greatness, then prepare for your destiny!** Google Search: "Greatness is not a Coincidence"! Do not wait for Greatness to arrive to prepare because your lack of preparation or procrastination could result in less than great results. Prepare for Greatness and your efforts & preparation will attract Greatness! ***The biggest proponent to***

success is "FEAR"\ False Evidence Appearing Real. I remember a few times in my sports career as a Coach that we as a staff on a couple of teams went into a few games believing that we were going to get our hat handed to us because of lack of this or they had that or differences in development of personnel. As a player I never had this problem because I was always taught to ***be a Leader & a difference maker, to always play to win & to Hit Hard and Never Quit!*** Instilled in me were certain principles that I still utilize in my philosophy today such as ***"A Winner is not a quitter and a quitter is not a Winner"; "You'll Win if You Don't Quit", "There's no "I" in TEAM, but there is 1 in Champion & 2 in CHAMPIONSHIP!"*** We were taught to believe in what we were doing and to visualize being successful/achieving our goals. We were taught to always have a Positive Mental Attitude & that if we didn't believe that we could win to not show up for the game! If you can't help the team, don't hurt the TEAM! It is better to have a few with earnest efforts than to have many with lukewarm enthusiasm!

Now that you have your mind right or in the right frame of mind **to be $uccessful, YOU HAVE TO PUT IN SOME WORK!**

"All Hard Work leads to Profit, Mere talk only leads to Poverty"-Proverbs 14:23

The only place in life where "Success" comes before "Work" is in the dictionary! **You must have a "Willingness" to do what is required!**

**A lot of people knock Multi-Level Marketing (and it's not for everybody) but a lot of people have profited nicely and came up as a result of tying in with the right organization/ upline. In most cases they have quality products or services that serve to enhance life, save money and make money. (Look at the countless amounts of success stories of people who were "down & out" and then came up by joining: Amway, Avon, Mary Kay, 5-Linx, Noni, Kyani, Prepaid Legal, Visalis, World Ventures and countless others?) These businesses usually are a legal and honest side-hustle not to mention the vast amount of new contacts & concepts that you can come across to cross promote/"Piggyback" with your business. Imagine networking and exchanging business cards with a group of pre-motivated individuals at their seminars/meetings and then introducing them to your products & services? I love getting invited to go to network marketing meetings and seminars because you are going to come into contact with a group of new prospects with an open mind and open checkbooks looking for the next Great Thing which is YOU!

-SUCCESS Magazine came up strictly off of marketing to Multi-Level Marketing companies. They "tailor-make" a monthly/quarterly magazine for all of the top-level Multi-Level companies that positions & promotes the individual subscribing company as the best thing going and use them to attract/sign new recruits unbeknownst to them is that the competing Multi-Level company in the next ballroom has a similar version with their company positioned higher in some statistical category.

Readers Are Leaders!

"You can tell where a person is going by what he reads."

"Blessed is the man who finds wisdom, the man who gains understanding."-Proverbs 3:13

"When you have Excellent command of the English language, you can talk up on you some money!" – Big Ray

Start building your "Success & Wealth Library". *Whatever you want to do, or for whatever you want to become, they have a book/books on it!* ***Open the book! Read the book! Read a Chapter each night towards bettering yourself or your situation.*** *Utilize the information that can help you and leave the information that can't help you in the book.* Just because it can't help you now, doesn't mean that it won't be able to help you in the future when you get up to another level. **The first book that we recommend is a Bible.** It is a life map, unfolds secrets and has answers to every problem known to man. You just have to read, interpret, decipher and ***apply the principles within***. Study the Proverbs to obtain wisdom. Make sure you also study up on JESUS and the obstacles and situations that he had to face including how he chose to deal with them. Also research Solomon, one of the strongest & richest men who ever lived. Take note of his success stories and his downfalls and utilize them to your benefit.

Don't let anything or anyone distract you from gaining the knowledge that you need to be successful.

"In Jesus Name I Win, in the game of Life, AMEN!"

Recommended Readings List

*Readers are Leaders! With that being said, we have listed some books below {for informational & reference purposes only} that may help you improve quality of life, work through challenging situations or spearhead/jumpstart creative ideas to come up with solutions to your situations. Stay objective and keep an open mind. Don't always judge a book by its cover or its title. We do not subscribe to nor endorse all of the concepts or ideas listed in all of the books, nor are the opinions contained in them necessarily the opinion of this author.

RECOMMENDED READINGS LIST

50+ AUTHORS & BOOKS THAT YOU MAY WANT TO ADD TO YOUR WEALTH LIBRARY:

"Education is the most Powerful weapon which you could use to change the world."-Nelson Mandela

"90% of most Businesses failed because they quit or they had no marketing plan."-Armani Valentino

"80% of your success is going to be achieved by you showing up and being busy."-Armani Valentino

"You cannot solve a problem from the same consciousness that caused it. You must see the world anew."-Albert Einstein

Some of these Authors & Books will deal with variety and a myriad of topics and subjects that you will encounter as you matriculate in this process called Life. Some will deal with Spirituality, Relationships, Finances, Leadership, Strategy, and The Game of Life in itself to help you to achieve a Balance or Equilibrium if you will and ultimately your Goals in Life. In order to Win in the Game of Life, it would behoove you to know and be aware of various facets and not take a one sided approach so that you can recognize pitfalls and deal with them accordingly or avoid them all together.

In the Sports arena we were taught to not only learn the Offensive, Defensive and Special Teams {or Tactics} side of the Game, but the Business side as well so that one day you can become a "PRODUCER" instead of a "Consumer" or a "Consumable" COMMODITY. There's a Lesson to be learned from everyone {even if it's not to make the same mistakes that they have in the past to avoid bumping your head. In Sports, we would watch film on ourselves as well as of our opponents on a Regular basis and often times would roll the film back so that we could detect errors, correct mistakes and game plan adequately against the opposition.

There will be times in Life when in order for you to be Successful you will have to develop a competitive advantage which will sometimes include studying the competition or opposition to monitor and notate their tendencies, strategies and mindsets in the guise of game-planning and preparation to achieve optimal results. With that being said, some of the authors on this list may not be a "crowd favorite", but take note: "Favor is not always Fair!" How will you equip yourself for competition or opposition if you don't know or have knowledge of what it is that you're opposing nor whom it is that you're competing against; Sometimes it may be strongholds or principalities. Other times it may a man in an opposite colored uniform or the business across the street.

With knowledge being the new currency, it is better to be on top of your game, instead of the Game being on top of You! The Bible makes reference to "The People shall perish for a lack of knowledge" *Hosea 4:6* . In order to put on the "Full Armor" and fully equip yourself for the task at hand Ephesians

6:11 , its best to be knowledgeable in the arena of which you're competing to eliminate errors and mistakes.

***Special Note: R.I.F READING IS FUNDAMENTAL.**

As you pull up and research some of these authors, Remember, "Do not judge a book by its cover or its Title. Most of these authors have more books & literary works than the few that we have listed. Feel free to pursue deeper if you so desire. All of the theories presented in these books and/or manuscripts do not necessarily reflect those of the author of this article nor the publisher and are to be referenced for entertainment purposes only. The information contained in these articles & books are not to be construed as Financial nor Medical Advice from the author and if you need guidance or advice to seek the services of a bona fide spiritual leader, a certified financial advisor or a professional health care practitioner .

*THE BIBLE

*ROBERT T. KIYOSAKI, RICH DAD/ POOR DAD SERIES

*JEFFREY GITOMER The Little Black Book of Connections & The Little Platinum Book of "Cha-Ching"

*JAY CONRAD LEVINSON www.GuerillaMarketing.com

*T.D. JAKES "Before You Do", "Reposition Yourself" & "Maximize The Moment"

*JERRY JONES Playing to Win

*HANK SEITZ "Think, Feel & Grow Rich" & "The Happiest Man in the World"

*MIKE MURDOCK "Enjoy The Winning Life" & "Wisdom for Wining" + Many More! www.WISDOMONLINE.COM

*ARMANI VALENTINO "Business Warfare" www.ArmaniValentino.com

*SUN TZU

*MARY COLBERT 13-Women That You Should "NEVER" Marry

*TARIQ NASHEED The Elite Way

*ROBERT GREENE

*RAY HARDY "The 7-Figure/ Million Dollar Side Hustle" & "The 48-Laws of Winning"

*WALT FRAZIER The Game Within The Game

*KAREN RAMSEY Everything You Know About Money Is WRONG.

*ANDREW LECKEY The Lack of Money Is the Root of All Evil

*DAVID J. SCHWARTZ The Magic of Thinking Big

*JALEN ROSE Got To Give The People What They Want.

*THOMAS J. STANLEY & WILLIAM D. DANKO "The Millionaire Next Door" & "The Millionaire Mind"

*RAY LINDER What Will I Do With My Money

*C. THOMAS ANDERSON Becoming a Millionaire God's Way

*GARY V. WHETSTONE It only Takes One

*KEN IVY The Art of Human Chess

*JERRY R. WILSON 151-QUICK IDEAS to Get New Customers

*STEPHEN R. COVEY The 7-Habits of Highly Effective People

*RANDALL LANE P.O.V. LIVING LARGE

*DWIGHT NICHOLS GOD'S PLANS FOR YOUR FINANCES

*GRANT TEAFF A COACH'S INFLUENCE/ BEYOND THE GAME

*DON SPEARS

*LEWIS H. WILLIAMS III www.iHustleNation.com

*GEORGE S. CLASON THE RICHEST MAN IN BABYLON

*JOSHUA PIVEN & DAVID BORGENICHT THE WORST-CASE SCENARIO Survival Handbook

*CRISWELL FREEMAN

*BARBOUR Armed and Dangerous

*DONALD TRUMP " The Art of the Comeback" & "How To Get Rich"

*REGINALD GRANT "Success Stories,..."

*RENNEY MCLEAN ETERNITY INVADING TIME

*EARVIN "MAGIC" JOHNSON 32 WAYS TO BE A CHAMPION IN BUSINESS

*DWIGHT PATE I THINK I THOUGHT I KNEW!

*DALE CARNEGIE HOW TO WIN FRIENDS AND INFLUENCE PEOPLE

*BLAINE PARDOE CUBICAL WAREFARE

*"GAME CHANGERS The World's Leading Entrepreneurs: HOW THEY'RE CHANGING THE GAME & YOU CAN TOO!

*ILYCE R. GLINK 100 QUESTIONS EVERY FIRST-TIME HOME BUYER SHOULD ASK

*JOHN SPOLESTRA MARKETING OUTRAGEOUSLY

*ANDREW J. SHERMAN RAISING CAPITAL

*BRIAN GRAHM GET HIRED FAST

*JOE GIRARD MASTERING YOUR WAY TO THE TOP

*NATE ROSENBLATT ENCYLOPEDIA OF MONEY MAKING $ALES LETTERS

*KEVIN TRUDEAU "FREE MONEY "THEY DON'T WANT YOU TO KNOW ABOUT" & MANY MORE!

*YOHA LEM Thinking Out of The Box

*MICHAEL CORBETT THE 33 RUTHLESS RULES OF LOCAL ADVERTISING

*BARRY CALLEN PERFECT PHRASES for SALES AND MARKETING COPY

*BOB BEAUDINE THE POWER OF WHO!

*MICHAEL MACCAMBRIDGE THE FRANCHISE

*DAN SCHAWBEL ME 2.0 BUILD A POWERFUL BRAND TO ACHIEVE CAREER SUCCESS

*JOHN JANTSCH The Referral Engine: Teaching Your Business to Market Itself

*GREG MCKEOWN ESSENTIALISM

Special Notes: *The **less you make, the more you need to study! If you don't have at least***

50k minimum in your portfolio, savings or 401k, you don't need to watch TV more than 10-12 hours a week. The time used to be entertained can be better utilized to research, enrich or better secure your situation.

"Study to show thyself approved unto God, a workman who needeth not to be ashamed, rightly dividing the word of truth"-2 Timothy 2:15

STAYING MOTIVATED IN THE MIDST OF MAKING CHANGE FOR THE BETTER-

Sometimes in the midst of making "***Changes for the Better***"; "*Making Millions*", "*Making Champions*" or "*Major Chess Moves*" there may come moments or times in your life where you may run into or across what is called a "*slump*", a "*Rut*" or a "*Mental Block*" per say or even "*states of depression*" when things get tight or are not going right. It is during times like these when you need to revisit and review your written "*Goals & Aspirations*" in addition to updating your "*Vision Board*" to remind yourself of "***Why***" you are doing this in the first place. Remember that not all things that are worthwhile in Life are not always a "*Sprint*" or an "*Overnight Sensation*" but more so a "*Marathon*" or a "*Journey*". Anything worth having is worth working for. *Read Proverbs 14:23*

"90% of most Businesses failed because they quit or they had no marketing plan."-Armani Valentino

"80% of your success is going to be achieved by you showing up and being busy."-Armani Valentino

Also remember to work *"Smarter"* in addition to *"Harder"* and keep your eyes on the prize and stay focused. For those times when it may seem that you're lacking in "***Motivation, Inspiration or Encouragement***", you have to find those things that make you happy without causing a hindrance and surround yourself with it or put in front of you.

"***When you have an Elephant sized Vision, you can't have mosquito faith!"-****Big Ray*

"True Happiness comes from up above and from within"-Big Ray

*Go to Church, get a good workout in, listen to your favorite music that motivates you or go hit a comedy show, concert or play to get your mind moving or flowing. Also look at switching up your diet to more natural energy rich foods, fruits and vegetables. For those times when you need a quick *"Pick-me-up"* or a sudden change of mindset try a shot of Organic Apple Cider vinegar, Pure/ Tart Cranberry Juice & Reconstituted Lemon Juice to cleanse your body of toxins that may be blocking your creative flow. Sometimes when challenges arise, its best to check and see what's on the inside before you start looking for external causes.

Motivation comes in many shapes, forms and fashions. Whatever it takes to get your *"Creative Juices"* to flowing "**FULL-THROTTLE**" , You have to find that "***Personal LIKE-Button***" and push it as many times as necessary to pump, prime or "*Jump-start*" your enthusiasm. Whether you're in the midst of "Making Millions" or "Making Champions", some motivational factors may differ while others may remain the same. Below we have listed some "*News that you can use" for intellectual stimulation to change your situation in regards to Mental & Spiritual elevation."*

-TRIP/ VACATION OR CRUISE

- CHANGE YOUR LOCATION OR OCCUPATION

-SURROUND YOURSELF WITH PEOPLE THAT ARE "ENEMIES OF YOUR WEAKNESSES"

-CHANGE YOUR ATMOSPHERE

-CHANGE YOUR SHOES/ NEW WARDROBE

-TEST DRIVE DREAM CAR OR NEW VEHICLE

-GO TO THE BOOKSTORE AT THE MALL

-LISTEN TO YOUR FAVORITE MUSIC AND/OR UPGRADE YOUR AUDIO SYSYTEM

<u>*Special Note:</u> *If your main motivation in Life is obtaining "Material Things" or "Monetary" then be mentally prepared for the "Humpty-Dumpty" effect if you don't have balance or a proper "Life" perspective for those times when "Life" challenges do appear or sudden shifts of the market or economy take place.*

****Disclaimer: Check with your doctor before you begin any exercise regimen/program, diet or supplemental products! Furthermore, any supplements, exercise regimens, products or services listed in this publication are for example purposes only, not endorsed by the author or publisher and to be used at your own discretion.***

Chapter 51

The Acknowledgements Chapter: aka

"The Treasure Chapter

With Success in Life being a Team-Effort, I would like to say that I didn't get here by myself and would like to give credit where credit is due. First and foremost I thank GOD for his son JESUS, his Word and for protecting (from the seen & un-seen) & providing for me! Without him, I am nothing. I am giving GOD The Glory for choosing & giving me the strength, wisdom, guidance, knowledge and the experiences to write this book. (Mathew 22:14, Proverbs 14:23 & Mathew 6:21)

"To them that much is given, much be required." In my never ending quest for Success and my relentless pursuit of Excellence (even against insurmountable odds) I can sometimes seem demanding as well as insensitive to mediocrity, complacency & incompetence. For those on my team as well as those that I have encountered along this journey called life (even some of the haters because everybody plays an important part in the ecosystem) I always wanted the Best for US and have nothing but Love for YOU! {When you Love somebody or something, you will go above & beyond to make sure that they are successful or to help them to survive.}* *"Everybody Loves a Winner"*** *(except for the one* *that just lost, got cut or traded before the playoffs!) If you don't see your name listed in this section don't be upset, just be more productive & proactive in your life as well as mine. (Get with me on the side & we'll see if we can get you listed in the next book, plenty more to come. We had to get this one out to the printer before the year end!)*

In our philosophy of empowering and sharing the wealth with those who helped us to acquire it, we are promoting and giving back to some of those who have helped us along this journey called Life. If you see yourself listed consider yourself blessed as well as a Blessing. Highlight yourself and show it to your friends & family then tell 10-people to buy a book. If you see someone listed that has a business and you are in need of their services or in their town, stop by and talk to them Quick! You'll be Surprised at what you might Get! Don't forget to spend some $ with them and ask for "The Big-Ray $pecial" or to mention that you were referred by Chosen One Sports.

****Imagine the Economic Impact that could be made if just 300 of you would spend just a mere $10-20 a month with each of the following entities/businesses listed in this chapter on essential services or products that you were going to utilize or acquire anyway + save $ and get more bang for your "buck" ?*** *Sometimes in the guise of making $ or saving $ which both make sense you have to give {sowing $} in order to Receive. If you took a look at the* *average cost of acquiring a new customer/client which averages between $28-$42 each on the low end & up to $128-$242+ to attract higher end clientele, you come out much better spending some $ with someone that can return the favor and not get taxed like you're a resident of 2-countries.*

I would like to give thanks to my family {Parents, siblings, Grand Parents(RIP), Aunts, Uncles, Nephews, Nieces, Cousins & extended families) starting with one of the Greatest Life Coaches & Financial Planners of my time, my Father Ronald Hardy who also happens to have 2-Collegiate & 2-State Championships under his belt.

**I would also like to thank my Beautiful Mother Dorothy Hardy who was a Campus Queen and a Champion at Academic Games who taught me the importance of showing up for work or practice on time or before time!*

*I would like to acknowledge my Great Brother Ram Ram-Jam Sports & Entertainment who started winning at a young age and now as an adult is instrumental in helping several well known Actors, Entertainers, Boxers & World Champion Athletes reach their pinnacle and peak in their careers as a result of his association with them in addition to his affiliation with several NBA Championship teams in addition to Coaching & mentoring youth in High School and on the AAU teams that he sponsors to go to National Tournaments & Championships every year.

*Special Credit goes out to my Great Sister Rhonda who is in my estimation "***one of The Greatest Sisters that ever walked the planet.***" We would like to thank her for her countless hours of consultation that her firm has donated and invested into this project as well as what they have sowed into my life. Speaking of Credit, she can help you to clean your credit up in 3-6 months and have you "rolling right" & "*smelling like a rose"{Thanks for the hook-up on the S-Class. The Mansion is coming next.*

*Special Shout-Out to my Nephew of the Year Kharon www.AppleTradeUSA & www.ElectronicTradeUSA.com for keeping me up to date on the latest communication & electronic devices and for hooking me and my players up on how to get the High-end luxury autos at "The Players Price"! *We started him out early in life on these concepts and he came up nicely! He used to make $150-250 daily selling candy in Middle School & High School and had 2 cars by the age of 14 + the money to get someone to chauffeur him around until he got a license. He parlayed these funds and invested in a landscaping/snow removal company with 5 employees in addition to a mobile detailing business with the pressure washer built inside of the truck of which he sold the business for $25k after his 2nd year of college to concentrate more on his studies. He is also known as a talented web developer who can put your message in the atmosphere with no fear.*

*For those that like sports keep an eye out for my MVP-nephew Amauri *www.AmauriMVP.com* who has amazed Basketball fans nationwide since he was a toddler! Now highly ranked as one of the top Basketball players in the country he's being recruited & scouted by most major programs (as well as the PROS) and up for the Mr. Basketball award 2017'. http://rayforddevteam.neocities.org/

*Special Recognition goes out to my gorgeous niece Kiara aka *"Pretty Baby Ki-ki"* with Rayford Investments in Miami who has been applying a lot of the concepts listed in this book. (She is also the owner of "Ki-ki La-LA" Salon & Immaculate Cleaning Services of Detroit with over 35 employees). *Not bad for someone who was making 6-figures before the age of 22!* {Now her new nickname is *"Money-making Pretty Baby Ki-ki!"*

Although there are many who have contributed to my success (to many to notate or mention) I would like to give special thanks to some who have had concentrated efforts in helping me in my ascension towards greatness, because I didn't get here by myself.

*The Hardy Family, The Jones Family, The Benifield Family, The Sharpe Family & all the rest of my family world-wide!

*The Wong Family Faith-Image Consultant @ The Faith Touch-B.R., La & LA, Ca, Cy & Betty-RIP www.TheFAITHTouch.com

*The Hill family Winston, Fannie, Chip, Wendell & Whitney,

*The Suber Family especially Dorothy Suber-RIP who taught me the importance of having a Product & a Service at a young age.

*The Calloway Family;

*The Hamlin Family- Angie @ Hamlin BBQ & Strictly Sportswear Who inspired me to "Up my Game" & move a volume of products to make more in addition to dress to be the Best! Kathy @ Strictly Sportswear-Detroit, Mi who is a Legend in the Game and has been outfitting "Players, Ballers, Athletes & Entertainers for Decades; & Dr. Calvin Hamlin who can show you how to make sense out of nonsense;

*The Ballards,

*The Carnes Family-The Best Neighbors we ever had!

*Victor "Vic" Adams ***One of the Greatest Talent Scouts Ever!*** I patterned part of my game from observing him as I grew up. Whenever I needed a new school/college to attend, he always had one waiting in the wings! He and his boy ***Noel Brown*** are partially responsible for me completing my College education and I am forever Grateful.

*The Horatio William Foundation- It's always good to have a philanthropist on your team! www.HoratioWilliamsFoundation.org

*Rev. Tyrone Hannah & Family + Cornerstone Christian Fellowship-The Colony, TX,

*Pastor Ralph N. Moore Victory & Power Ministries-B.R, La. & WPFC-Radio. www.DrRalphMoore.com & www.wpfc1550am.com This man taught us the importance of Victorious living and strongly emphasized the principles of: Accountability, Responsibility & Discipline. He encouraged entrepreneurship and for everybody in the congregation to support one another's businesses. Check out his books on his website.

*Bishop T.D. Jakes- The Potter's House-Dallas, TX www.ThePottersHouse.org Check out his books including "Reposition Yourself", "Before You Do" & "Maximize the Moment".

*Pastors Joseph & Dr. Bridgette Steib- The Ministry of Love-B.R., La. www.MinistryOfLove.com

*Coach Earnest Thomas-RIP- Who taught us the power of Thinking Big & Visualizing Success!

*Coach James Anderson Thanks for helping me and a lot of my players with our financial aid. Due to your assistance, mentoring & coaching, college was definitely some of the Best Days of our Lives!

*Scott Bradford aka "Big-Scott"-RIP A TRUE CHAMPION

*Cousin Harry Jones with "Harry's Ribs & Chicken"-Detroit MI.

*The Mackey Family- Robert, Jackie & Roderick;

*The Higgins Family Brian, Regina & BJ;

*Everetta Edwards- If you need marketing/publicity for your product, service or events, their company can pump you up like the "Old-school Reeboks" www.KustomEvents.com . If you're in need of a "Press-Conference" or "Draft-Day" Suit, get at her for custom tailored looks at the Team Rate or Player's Price! Check out Everlux Custom Clothiers: www.EverLux.net D.C., Miami. If your order is substantial, they can even fly in & size you up with a deposit;

Keegan McIntosh, Les Brown, Mike Hill, Ken Davis,

*The Lake Highlands Wildcats Youth Association www.LHWYA.COM { Coach Mackey & Mrs. Mackey, Coach Mike Nixon, Coach Dre' Andre Young, Coach Hall "Everybody Loves a Winner", Coach Derrick Tyler & The Wildcats Fans & Family who helped us to Win Those Bowl-Games, Championships & Tournaments.

* Kevin Lloyd-Director of the Earl Lloyd Foundation. When I was in college, he helped me to transition from *"one HU to the Next"* in addition to enlightening me on school, life, entrepreneurship and networking. Currently, he is working in conjunction with the NBA to carry on the Legacy of his father Earl Lloyd-RIP who was the first African American to play and coach in the NBA.

*Andy Brown author & Radio Personality www.AndyBrownSpeaks.com ; www.TheOnlineHappyHour.com & www.iLifeRadio.com

*Kevin Hopwood & J.R. The Mastermind behind "TMi-Media Group" www.TMiRadio.com "Global, National & Local". When you have music or a message that you need to go around the world, this is one of the places that you want to utilize to get it there. ,

*Dewayne Bryant- owner of the Ten-11 Grill-Dallas, TX www.TenElevenGrill.com ,

*Robert Pierce www.CarnivoXO.com ,

*The Mims Family Brothers Garnett www.MusclesInMotionSystems.com ; www.LinemenOnly.com ; Publicist David aka "Daveed" with Det2LA.com & the marketing firm of Mims & Nem "Making It Mean Something"; + their nephew Jamone;

*REGINALD GRANT-MS-Ed. The founder of the Grant Language Academy, this guy is multi-faceted & multi-talented & He wears many hats such as a Professor, Instructor, Coach, Author, Entrepreneur, and Philanthropist. He is a noted Speaker on the Lecture circuit who is well connected & respected Nationwide who was instrumental in me getting some of my manuscripts out. Check out his new book 'Success Stories" and look him up online www.ReginaldGrant.com ;

www.AFamilyOfAuthors.com ; www.GrantLanguageAcademy.com ; www.eSportsInstruction.com

*Joan Louis- An innovator and a Trend-setter in the Hair Industry who showed me how to tap into a Billion dollar industry & come out with an adequate piece of the pie. Owner of MoHair Salon-Baton Rouge, La. www.MoHairOnline.com

*Michael Towns www.WhoIsMichaelTowns.com &The Twins You know who you are! ,

*"Rocki" Raquel Sawyer President of Detroiters in Dallas. It's amazing how you put this thing together & keeps it running smoothly with so many complex & diverse personalities;

Nathaniel "Gooney" Hampton, Bridget Small, Big-Duke, Charles Hearns-,

* Adrian Harris Thanks for helping the vision to manifest!

*Adrian Miller & Family Owner of Sweet-Sweet-backs Bad Azz Bones & Dirty Mac's BBQ-Ft.Worth, TX; He has that flavor that you savor & that "killer-sauce"!

*Robert Williamson & his sister Sandra;

*Pastor Freddie Haynes Friendship West Baptist Church-Dallas, Texas www.friendshipwest.org

*Ocie Taylor with Taylor's Floors in Ft. Worth, TX He puts it down with Precision! Quality Work at a Reasonable Price! www.TaylorFlooringTx.com

*Terry Sullivan www.AllAmericanBowl.com ,

*Amber Davies- A female that's making an impact in a man's game with the NFL-Houston Texans Scouting Dept. www.HoustonTexans.com ,

*Armani Valentino- author/Motivational Speaker & owner of College Boy Publishing www.ArmaniValentino.com ,

*Arnold Nevels, Arnold "Darnel" Woods, Howard Fanning, Steve Harvey, Bernie Mac-RIP; Robyn Buchanan,

*Angela Williams-The owner of Dorroyz Hair Loss Solutions in Arlington, TX has helped men, women & children with hair loss issues grow healthy hair using non-surgical_methods.
www.DorroyzHairLossSolutions.com

* Comedian Anastasia "The Bold" Bolden' she's one of the top female comedians in the DFW-Metroplex that will definitely get an audience's attention. www.AnastasiaTheBold.com

*Shemeika Wright- Wrightway Tax Services-Dallas, Texas. "*Where you can get your taxes done the Wright-way*" www.wrightwaytaxservices.net

Coach Andy Hispher, Coach Damon Stodimire- He was also "Cold-Blooded as a Player!' Coach Mike Barrow, Coach Doug Smiley,

*My boy "Big-Charles" Charles Wynn the gospel percussionist;

*Dimetria Wright -Wright Legal Services -B.R., La. They can help you to go from *"Hot Water"* to a fresh cup of tea for a small fee!

*Coach Eric Jones-aka "Big-E"; who is one of the most prolific and inspirational Coaches & D-Line trainers in Texas. He stresses the importance of *"Putting yourself in position to Win!"*

*Coach Brad Frazier
www.OldSchoolQuarterbacks.com ,

*Coach Blake Frazier-CFL-Scout for the Roughriders & JC-Coaching Legend who is One of the 2 football guru's that I consult when going up against a formidable opponent to set game plans to shut them down like K-mart or dissect them like a frog in Biology class. ,

*Coach Wilfred Thomas- who helped me to set an indoor scoring Record in the All American Bowl in addition to instilling in me a phrase that I utilize in my daily walk. "Yeah though I walk through the Valley of The Shadow of Death, I will fear no Evil. WHY? BECAUSE I'M THE BADDEST CAT IN THE JUNGLE!"

*Coach Rodney Blackshear- Former Texas Tech great and AFL-Iron-man, now One of the Great Offensive Minds in the game of Football. He has taken arena routes & applied them to the 11-man game with astounding results,

*Coach Curtis Blackwell One of the top College Recruiting Coordinators & developers of talent in the country with Sound Mind/Sound Body Football Camps which attracts the Top Football Players & College Coaches from all over America. www.SMSBcamp.com

*Coach Les Miles I appreciate you for coming in to present me with the Nike Coach of the Year Award www.LesMiles.com

*Coach Frank Wilson in every major program there is a coach behind the scenes that helps to make things go Great & he is one of them! Now that his hard work has paid off, he has been catapulted into the forefront as a leader of his own program

*Coach Nick Saban All he does is WIN, wherever he goes! He also has one of the most intense Football Camps in the Country.

*Coach Bobby Wilson another coach behind the scenes, who helps to propel his program to National Championships,

*Coach Gary Patterson an intense coach with a passion for perfection & one of the few to ever have a perfect season 12-0;

*Mike Sinqfield- Director of Football Operations at TCU

*Coach Tommie Robinson Wherever he goes, College or PRO he is producing Results & coming out on Top,

*Coach Will Martin-Check out his DVD for DB's on www.CoachesChoice.com ,

*Cedric Fails-Accountant and Owner of C.G. Fails & Associates Accounting Firm-Detroit, Mi. where they keep your books tight & your money Right! www.CGFails.com ;

*Gerald Wade Financial Analyst with the Coca-Cola bottling company of Atlanta.

*Derrick Vaughn aka "DJ-Chill" www.IamBossmanDino.com

*Coach Christian Vitale www.TheKickIsUp.com

*Maurice Stokes-aka Mo-Tickets & Mo-Cars-Dallas, TX;

*Roy Tarpley-RIP former schoolmate & NBA 6th man of the year;

Tim Autry-The Ultimate Realtor, Tina Cooper-Tyler & Family;

*Todd Cadwallader Premier Youth Football League www.PYFL.com

*Ms. Dorris Pacific Island Athletic Association;

*Hassan Barzani- One of the Best Interns that we've ever had! It's time to make that money! You need your own Product Line!

*Barbara Thompson, Coach Willie Tyson,

*Joy Stephens www.kidswellcare.com; www.t30andbeyond.com

* Nicole Johnson- Owner-Hands of Glory Salon-Dallas, TX www.HandsOfGlorySalon.net

*Gene Thrash- The owner of Corganics Inc, has a Great Product called "RELIEF" and it really works! One of his associates had approached us about marketing/promotions for the company & gave us some samples. A few days later I incurred a freak accident getting out of the shower and ended up having a knee injury. Long story short, I ended up using the product and am now a customer as well! www.Corganics.com

*Bret Cooper-The Director of the Junior Academic All-American Bowl & the High School All-American game who creates opportunities for youth nationwide. Well Connected, Well Respected. Often Imitated, never duplicated, he has set the bar in Youth Sports & All-Star Games. www.BretCooperFootball.com

*Marshal Fortson 5-LINX , Steve Carter 5-LINX & ID-Life , Lee Lemons 5-LINX ,Catherine Harvey 5-LINX ,Reginald Edwards 5-LINX, Rosa Battle 5-LINX

,Thomas McLemore NFL-Detroit & Indianapolis, Jimmy Johnson NFL,

*Chris Scott Sr. & Jr.

*William Kareem Baker One of the up & coming Sports video filming editors with "Phenom World Sports"

*Tony Stephens Primerica, Urshula Udics, Coach Hugo Hughes

*Kevin Burrell & Family

*Cheron K. Griffin author & host Reality TV show "Preachers Ex'es" www.CheronKGriffin.com ,

*Pastor Renney McClean & Family Check out his book "Eternity Evading Time", www.RMMinistries.com

*Pastor Bill Earley,

*Pastor Gene Peyton,

*Dr. Mike Murdock-Ft. Worth, TX His books, DVD's & Lectures have inspired me to reach additional levels of Greatness & overcome obstacles, but has helped a lot of my Players & Coaches as well. I usually take a couple of his books with me when I travel, especially to the Big Games & I always happen to bump into him at the airport as he travels spreading the Good News of JESUS CHRIST and helping people to break the back of poverty. His messages impart so much knowledge & wisdom that

they can elevate your Spirit, your mind and your bank account if you let it. www.WisdomCenter.cc ;

The Late Gerald Levert,-RIP; The Late Emanuel Steward-RIP; Brian McKnight; Kem, Damien Butler Owner of The North Texas Express & Sports agent.

*Caesar with www.DALLASGospelConnection.com & The Pipkin Law firm has helped several of my clients come up like the Jefferson's & live like Jed Clampet in the Beverly Hillbilly's!

*Denise Joyner, www.exclusif-e.com;

*Mary Pierce & her son Donte www.UrHappyHouse.com ,

*Rev. Henry Parker Ark. Baptist Univ. , Evangelist Yundrae Wilson, Suebe Herring,

*Michael McDonald aka "Big-Mike"-European Basketball Player & Event Promoter–Dallas, TX www.BigMikeEvents.com

*Luther Coppage A Master Strategist & VP of www.LucysLingerie.com based in Beverly Hills, Ca & Las Vegas, NV who showed me how to stay abreast of not only current, but future trends to stay ahead of the game & come out sweet smelling

*Craig Spruill with Playmaker Sports Marketing www.PLYMKRSSPRTS.COM

*Dr. Elizabeth Branch- she has an excellent concept for helping students & athletes to improve their

grades & test scores. Check out www.CollegeBoundBallerz.org

*Dr. Theodore B. Riley aka "Big-Ted"; Carolyn Miller aka "Cee Millions" with N Control Records; Robin Robinson;

*Lori Rambo aka Comedian "Sommore" She is one of the Original Queens of Comedy & considered one of America's top female entertainers; she has mystified fans & sold out venues nationwide. www.Sommore.com

*D. Elli$ Dallas King of Comedy aka Mr. Entertainment! The comedian-actor-musician is a "Triple-Threat" in the entertainment field and will have you coughing up a lung laughing. www.dEllisWorld.com

*Lavelle Crump aka "David Banner" Former schoolmate & SGA/ Student Body President turned Rapper, Actor & Music producer & Civil Rights Activist who literally carries the state of Mississippi on his back.

*Carlton Mosley aka "Cool-C" who set the Hair-World on fire and gave them chills at the same time with his ICE-Magazine & Product line, Beauty School & performances in Hair-Battles around the country. His hairstyles set world-wide trends of which many renowned hair-stylists patterned their game after. In high-demand as a host, speaker & instructor he set the bar in the Urban hair industry.

*Myra Brazile, "Bad-Boy"-Jermaine-Det. Mark Macon NBA,

*Maurice Smith @ Encore Salon-Southfield, Mi,

*Romel Russell aka Martez owner of Paparazzi & Imaginations Salons in B.R., La,

*George Hunt- The Owner of *"Tight-Fades"* Barbershop in B.R, La.

*DJ 4.0 www.fourpointohh.com .

*DJ Gary Chandler the World Renowned Turntable Technician at Hot 107.5 in Detroit who is still putting it down for the Crown. Early in my career, he and a few other DJ's were instrumental in drawing large crowds of epic proportions to my events that funded a portion of my college experience. This guy single handedly made a Restaurant Franchise the top selling unit in America with his music (and its still #1 for over a decade thanks to him.) If you want to make your music famous, pack a venue or supply the sounds that can stimulate your bank account, check out www.DJGARYCHANDLER.COM

*Special Shout-out to my boy Wan Ali originally from Chicago with Wan-Wear –Las Vegas, NV who custom makes our hats & apparel for major events & special occasions. Check him out www.WanWear.com & www.WanAli.com .We were down from day-1 since we met at the Superbowl in 98' and now he is a household name among the nation's elite athletes & entertainers. With "A-List" clients such as

Presidents, Senators, Mega-Superstars & more, if you need your campaign or wardrobe to be "*Outstanding*", he is the man with an outstanding wardrobe plan!

*Vincent Viott Mann- The other football guru that I consult when going up against a formidable opponent for Un-stoppable Offensive schemes that will allow me to open up the Offense like Wal-Mart franchises & Put points on the board like a Las Vegas slot machine. On Defense he is one of the originators who helped me to develop my own versions of "***The Gangster***" & "***The Worlds-Greatest***" Defenses that are designed to stop people in their tracks like glue style "*Rat-Traps*"! His Special Teams play mystifies opponents & keeps the fans in their seats. "Don't look behind you, because he might be in front of you"! Don't let the smooth taste fool you!

*Clarence Larry Jackson & Family Owner of CJ's Barber & Beauty Salon-B.R., La.

*Eric Fowler E's Tee's; The Late Michael "Bear" Taliaferro-RIP; The Late Lyle Alzado-RIP; Gregory Wade,

*The Late Al Davis-RIP Owner of the Oakland Raiders." Just Win Baby", He is still winning long after he's gone,

*Wyatt Harris- Director of
www.SonicBoomTraining.com A former teammate whose work ethic was unparalleled. He emphasized the importance of utilizing martial arts techniques to

give you an advantage over your opponents in sports and in life.

*Darren Deloatche-A No-Nonsense Sports Agent & Scout who gets you more "Bang for the Buck" www.AscensionEntInc.com ,

*Attorney Sadat Montgomery If you ever get *"Hit"* in an accident call or hit up Sadat and get what you deserve! www.214Deserve.com Dallas, TX. I like the way he has his phone # built in his web address! I wonder where he got that idea from?

*Atty. Dr. Harry Washington Ezim-B.R, La.

*Atty. Elvin Sterling-B.R., La. Not only was he tenacious on the field as a football player & Student Government President in college, He is tenacious in the courtroom as well. Also owner of Sterling construction where they can put it together in any kind of weather.

*Germaine 'Germany" Miller with Joasie Mae's Restaurant & Aunt-G's Pies in LA, Ca. & N.O., La.

*Kenneth Grover www.UndergroundRecruit.wordpress.com,

*Mike Fenske & Steve Lickman with MJF Football Recruiting www.MJFFootballRecruiting.com

*Brodrick Sublet This Former Arena Football Player & now Coach is also one of the Top HS Recruiting Coordinators in Dallas, TX is truly an asset to every program that he embraces.

*Ryan Johnson-One of the Top Promoters as well as one of the Top Male Hair Stylists in Dallas, TX www.Studio5012.com ;

*Fred Banks- aka "Casino" Promoter & CEO of World Wide Entertainment Group and *Owi-Events* based out of Dallas, TX who produces & promotes *"mind-boggling"* events. www.VIPofDallas.com & www.TruthNightClubDallas.com

*Chris Butler - The CEO of ICON-Entertainment Group. When you need an event developed, marketed or promoted, he's the man with the plan.

*Andre Lang aka *"Ft. Worth Dre"* Promoter & Graphic Artist-Fort Worth, Texas.

*Gregland Burns aka *"DeVille"* The Legendary Promoter and Creative Director of one of the most innovative Event marketing tools in Texas. Not only can he fill large auditoriums with a single "E-blast", he can make you or your event *"FAMOUS"* and an overnight sensation. www.PartyChaser.com

*Rume w/Devin the Dude Singer, Song-writer, Actor, Musician extraordinaire who has been putting in work on tours across America. http://www.RumeWorld.com

*Solomon Page Former NFL-Player with the Cowboys/Chargers and Founder of Step Into Excellence Motivational Speaking & Training.

*Todd Krueger-Elite QB Trainer & Coach www.PlayQB.com ,

Yusef Chew, Coach Farasi Norman, Glen "Big-Baby Davis-NBA; Antoine Joubert, Shaquille O'Neal, Shannon Murphy with The Making of Champions who gave me a whole new insight on Special Teams Play, Coach Maurice Burris, Coach Milton Wallace,

*Monja Qui with www.QuiEntertainment.com

*Coach Torlonzo Tate www.LouisianaEagles.com ,

Coach Marino Casem-"We don't reward losing", Coach Haynes Kenner Chiefs & the New Orleans Knights; Dr. Amber Banks, Roosevelt Johnson,

*Sydnee Turner –She has a passion for graphics like we have a passion for sports! www.SydGrafix.com

*Selwyn Harris at Classic BMW-PLANO, TX. Giving Exceptional Service and Reasonable Rates!

*Pedro over at www.VolvoOfDallas.com for the many miracles that they have worked to get people rolling for little or nothing down.

*Tammie Riggs-Former Bank Executive, Grant Writer & VP, now turned philanthropist who puts Student Athletes in touch with a good dose of *"Reality"* when it comes to Recruiting. ewww.StudentAthletesInTouch.com ,

*Tamara Goodwin {Actress & Model that gets the job done in good taste. www.TamaraGoodwin.com ;

*Larry Brown-NFL 94'Superbowl MVP www.MetroplexSelect.com and www.ColleyvilleCowboys.com .

*Mike "Scooter" McGruder NFL-49'ers/Patriots. Showed me how not to get fooled by elaborate passing schemes.

*Byron Williams President of the NFL-Players Association-Dallas Chapter & member of the 87' Super bowl Champs-NY-Giants who caught the Winning Touchdown. www.FootballMiniCamps.com Also hit him up if you need a stadium built or Tire Turf installed.

*Spud Webb former NBA-Dunk Champion & Current GM of The Texas Legends-NBA-D-League www.TexLegends.com

*Myles White-One of the Top-3 WR's to ever come through Chosen One Sports. NFL-Green Bay Packers/NY Giants & Jets who started 7 games as a Rookie the year after the Packers last Super Bowl victory.

*Lomas Brown NFL-HOF Detroit Lions

*Aeneas Williams NFL-HOF. One of my former team mates who is a testament that submitting to the Will of GOD and the authority of CHRIST along with hard work pays off. James 4:10 & Proverbs 14:23. He is an Achiever! He set goals and he accomplished them against insurmountable odds. Pick up a copy of his book "IT TAKES RESPECT". Also if you are ever in

Phoenix or St. Louis stop by one of his churches and take in a worship service.

*Maurice Hurst NFL-Patriots. Another one of my ex-Team mates who overcame insurmountable odds to make it and last 9 years on one of the toughest teams in the NFL, Currently working as an NFL Scout.

*Donald Fusilier-one of the Top-3 WR's to come through Chosen One Sports who overcame adverse obstacles in life and still persevered to produce optimal Results! A true student & now a Master of the Game who is a testament that "Hard work pays off, when channeled in the proper direction. Google search or look up on YouTube.com *"The Donald Fusilier Horror Show."* You will be AMAZED as he "Lights the Fuse"! Check out his book "The Donald Fusilier story."

* Thomas "Pepper" Johnson former High School & College All-American@ Ohio St. /All-PRO NFL-LB Giants, Jets, Lions, Patriots/Future HOF & Super-bowl Champion turned Coach who "Hit-Hard" every play! He taught me the important lesson early in my career to be careful of whom you let in your inner circle & that you can't hang out with everybody.

*Quentin McKinney "*The Dallas Legend*" is **The Best WR to never go PRO!** He is the equivalent of Basketball's Earl "The Goat" Manigoat for football. Google search him and look at the film on YouTube.com. I have seen this man score 6-

touchdowns in a game in all 3-phases of the Game: Offense, Defense & Special Teams. Now an instructor in the fine art of Football and mentor to many area athletes, he teaches proper techniques so that they can compete on the field and in Life as well.

*Terrence Mann aka "T-Mann"-the former All-American & Mr. Football in Michigan in addition to USA-Today Top-5. In college he was a stand-out for SMU during the Glory Days! Drafted by the Dolphins, He was one of the Top-2 Nose-guards that I ever had to go up against. He was instrumental in my development. After lining up in front of him for 3-years of High School Football & 3-years of Middle School Basketball, his graduation to go to college allowed me to become one of the Best Centers in Detroit & later on one of the Best in the Game!

*Isaac "Big-Ike" Readon NFL/CFL/former NCAA All-American & Div.2 Defensive Player of the Year 85' & Top-3 Rated NG in the draft coming out in 86. Ike is the other Top-NG that I had to go up against and learned a valuable lesson in life. He was a Beast on the Field and a Great Guy off the field. He introduced me to the Real World of College Football and helped me to get my mind right! I passed up going to Clemson because I was trying to avoid running into All-American Nose-guards namely William "The-Refrigerator" Perry & his brother Michael Dean Perry. I signed with a smaller college because I believed that I could go in there and dominate as opposed to sitting on a bench at a major college for 2 years. I was rudely awakened & introduced to the CIAA by Big-Ike as I found out that All-American Football Players came in all shapes, sizes & locations and that if I was ever going to achieve or accomplish anything in Life I had to face challenges head on and not run from them. One of the other lessons that I learned was that the game is 90% mental but on that last 10% you have to put in some work & attack the weights. After 4-semesters in front of Ike, when he graduated & left, so did I. After going up against him, everything else was down hill. I decided that I was made to be "Big-Time & transferred to a Bigger School and unleashed a Beast of my own. I purposed in my Heart that no Nose-Guard would ever get the best of me ever again in Life!

* Jerry B-all NFL-Detroit Lions/Vikings-This man was a force to be reckoned with. He was like a Pit-bull, not the biggest, but one of the most aggressive non-stop. Not only was he a physical player, but he had the mental game down as well. He would talk you out of your game if you let him. After a few years of hanging out at the Lions Pre-Season camps during my Collegiate Summer breaks I picked up on various techniques/traits that helped me to elevate my game.

*Darren "Sweet-D" Wilson USFL-LA-Avengers. He taught me the importance of always looking your best and to always keep your composure under pressure and to never let "them" see you sweat. An important aspect of Life that I learned from him was that if you are late, no amount of rushing or running will make you on time. Travel to arrive alive & sweet-smelling.

*Charles Edward Hugan aka "Big-Hurk"& "Hoagie" Steelers, Det. Buccaneers and Det. Seminoles: Thanks for teaching me Great techniques during the summer breaks and the significance of O-Line Play + the importance of Beating peoples behind on the line of scrimmage and to do it with a bad attitude. He took me under his wing and showed me how to use my hands and to develop to be a technician of the game. He was one of the founders of the Fraternal Order of Offensive Linemen F.O.O.L for short and we used to do just that, act a fool on the football field. We used to sing & dance and have a good time. Shout out to his brother Byron Culver too! He was a "Blocking Machine!"

*Coach Percy Duhe-RIP He taught us that *"If you want to be Great, You must do something Extra"!* Also, he emphasized to be careful of the company you keep and not to hang out with bums & drunkards.

*Coach Bill Mars Thanks for Believing in me and giving me an opportunity.

*Coach Willie Ponton *"Whatever you are lacking in talent you better make up for it with hard work"*!

*Coach Willie Jeffries One of the first African Americans to become a Head Football Coach at a Division 1 institution who taught us *"Whenever* *something goes wrong, make sure that you have a Reason and not an Excuse!"*

*Coach Tony Knox-The former All-American Center who became one of my OL coaches towards the end of my College career who was one of the few Centers alive that could stay in front of "Big-Ike" whom he played against in the All American game. He taught me important concepts about life and taking care of your family in addition to advanced techniques of how to shock up through the man in football + important lessons on perseverance.

*Coach Nick Calcutta-One of the Greatest OL coaches in America. This man showed me how to refine my pass-blocking as to where very few got past me after his tutelage. When I took my show on the road, they were amazed!

*The Penn Brothers- Coach William Penn-RIP & Coach Arthur Penn-RIP who owned Penn Sporting Goods and the Northwest Wolverines Youth Football Organization in Detroit, Michigan. They provided opportunities & guidance for many youths {including myself} and their entrepreneurial activities inspired many to continue on to higher education or greater heights.

*Coach Archie "Gunslinger" Cooley-One of the Architects of "The West-Coast" Offense who achieved fame for being the College Coach who made Jerry Rice Nice & also for selling his Offensive package to Bill Walsh of the San Francisco 49'ers who went on to set Records & Win Superbowls with it. Thanks for utilizing our services & for letting me hang around for a season to polish up my game and hone my offensive skills to now dissect Defenses like a frog in a Biology class.

*I want to thank all of the Coaches that were instrumental in my life & development. A lot of the concepts, ideas & philosophies that you helped to instill in me, are still being utilized to this day as well as passed down to generations to come to help produce "Winning Lifestyles."

*I want to thank all of my former teammates. {It was definitely a learning experience. **For those of you that got your behinds busted on the field of play {*"it's because you didn't attack the weights"*},** don't take it personal, it was business. I was just getting you ready for the Real-World and you can probably appreciate me now. What didn't kill you made you stronger? If not, as the Great Coach Casem used to say *"They can't take that a_-_ whipping off of them"* and you have to respect it! All I wanted to do was "***WIN***" and if you got in the way, all you became was part of that road that paved the way towards Greatness and becoming a Champion!

*To all of my former & future players: Without you, all of this wouldn't have been possible. Thanks for the Championships and the Championship Rings! Winning is definitely a Lifestyle! For those that didn't stay long enough to get a Ring: "A Winner is not a quitter and a Quitter is not a Winner! You'll WIN if you don't Quit (& get your mind Right!") **It's Real on the Field!** It's not *"Play-station or X-Box."* Most Important: "Keep Your Head on a Swivel on the field & in life because someone is always looking to take it off!" ***Stop the Excuses*** and put your mind to good use. "***A mind is a terrible thing to waste.***" Get in front of a mirror and repeat after me: "**Everyday I go to sleep as a Winner & wake up as a CHAMPION!**" If any of you ever need me, don't hesitate to reach out & contact me or call, because "***Teamwork makes the Dream Work***" & "***Success in Life is a Team Effort!"***

*Mr. Russell Chew Owner of Chew's Beauty Supply & Manufacturing who showed me the importance of flowing in the "*Spirit*" when making decisions in addition to showing me another level of the Business side of the "*Hair-Game*". As an intern with them during my college years I learned the importance of Distribution channels & connectivity.

"You can have the best product in America, but if no one knows that you exist or if you can't get the product to the people it will go undersold!"

Check out his annual International Hair Show www.ChewsHairAffair.com & get up his new signature air fragrance.

The Detroit Buccaneers, The Dallas Cowboys, The Detroit Lions, Shawn Johnson, Charles Wiley with Infinity Web Design, C.E. Wiley Studios & 504-Dymes-B.R., La. Coach Mike Tyson, Anthony Brooks

Scoops Barbershop, Kirk Anthony Jackson III aka "Big-Tre"-RIP, Coach Vanzant, Coach McClung, Kim Brown, Coach Robert Bishop, Danielle Fluker aka "The Princess", Carla McClatty,

*Coach & Trainer Sharee Thompson   Former SEC & European Basketball star, now one of the Top female Basketball & Fitness trainers in the DFW-Metroplex & Orlando who is serious about her craft. In the true sense of the word "Champion", she finds a way to Win. www.tSportsFit.com

*Coach Terrell Woody   He is a Trainer of some of the NBA's elite players & Draft prospects. He is also a Facilitator of the "Swisher-Courts" Sports Complex/ Athletic facility in Lewisville, Texas where they transform projects into legitimate prospects.

*Hampton University   This is A Beautiful Place. It is 3/5th surrounded by water & had me feeling like I was on "***Fantasy Island***". The Va. Beach & the Chesapeake Bay was stupendous. I definitely got a chance to experience how the Rich live and didn't want to give up that lifestyle. They were true to their image with all of the Beautiful & Intelligent people on campus. www.HamptonU.edu

*Howard University   They let you know Day-1 that you were "***Cream of the Crop***" & "***The Best of the Best***" and what a privilege it was to be enrolled here for every person enrolled, 10k had tried & applied! We were taught that it wasn't anything that we couldn't achieve or receive if we put our minds to it!

The main thing that I liked about this school was that creativity was encouraged and ***they didn't teach or train you to be a slave, graduate and always work for someone else, but more so to eventually take ownership of your situation*** and not to despise small beginnings. ***Academics came first*** and ***sports were actually an extracurricular activity*** and not a job. **They placed a "*Priority*" on Intelligence and the classroom setting was "*Highly Competitive*"** to say the least. ***Some of the most intelligent & elite individuals in the country have matriculated at this institution*** of higher learning. www.Howard.edu

*Southern University & A&M College This is a place that ***"Reigns Supreme in Sports" &*** *has* ***"One of The Best Bands in The Land"*** *due to the massive amounts of time, energy and effort* put into practice & preparation for these events. ***"They are Serious about the Product that they display or put upon The Field or Court of Play!"*** At Southern, If you can't *"cut the mustard", they will CUT YOU & Your $ Too! As one famous former Coach used to say "Cut-Away Holmes" or "You Better Get You Some Stay Here!" At first it was a culture shock*, but we learned how to adapt & adjust to overcome the obstacles of life in addition to dealing with the masses of the people. The cream will definitely rise to the Top! ***It was a true learning experience to get you ready for the real world.*** We learned to develop networking skills early on. It was evident that it wasn't always what or who you know, but more so to whom you are connected to and who knows you. www.SUBR.edu

*LSU Some of the Greatest Athletes that ever played the game wore Purple & Gold! This was one place where fan participation definitely played a role in the outcomes of some games! They don't call it "Death Valley" for nothing! Whenever the football team scored you could hear the roar & feel the vibrations like an earthquake miles away! www.LSU.edu

*Cooley High School-Detroit, Mi. **Home of The Champions!** *"Where the Strong Survive & the rest get eaten alive"!* This is where I learned the art of the "*Killer-Instinct*" mindset in athletics, academics & sometimes on my daily journey to school because Champions Always Find a Way to Win! We were taught to Win with class and have good sportsmanship but to also "*kill a knat with a sledge-hammer & to cut the rope when your opponent is hanging off of the cliff*!" The 5 or 6 teams that could say they won against us in a 4-year period never wanted to line up against or play us again nor were they ever the same after playing against us. Most of them took 2-3 weeks to recuperate or rehab from injuries after playing us. The training that I received here was similar to that of "Special-Forces" training which turned some of us into "*1-man army's or wrecking crews*". One on one, we were never to get beat by 1 man. The motto of the day was "*if you can't win, don't loose*" and I still operate by some of those same philosophies today.

*Professor Katrice Albert & Professor Barbara Thomas at Southern Univ.-BR. These 2-ladies helped me to develop into the Marketing Genius that I am today. After winning the *"Mr. Marketing"* award in 91' in the School of Business the sky was the limit after that! We also helped to develop *"T.T. Allain` Day" where everybody came to school fresh {due to the Recruiters we were attracting from major corporations} now known as "Pretty Wednesday" on campus which was also the inspiration for the hit song.*

*Professor Earl Marcelle at Southern Univ.-BR. He taught us the important concept of *"C.Y.A" Cover Your Assets* along with how to prepare and avoid the *"Games & Tricks"* that people play in Corporate America. The Valuable Lessons that he taught us were instrumental in my development.

*Agent & Atty. Tim Crawford All I can say is ***"Thoroughly Impressive" & THANK YOU!***

*Thomas "Hitman" Hearns aka "The Motor City Cobra" **6-time World Champion Boxer** who taught me that ***if you believe in yourself and what you are doing to invest time into yourself to be the best that you can be so that when opportunity presents itself you can be in a position to receive.***

*Shout-out to my future wife?

*Noel Scarlet Former NFL Player-Cowboys/Vikings who now Coaches, trains & prepares prospects for the combine & the next level. When the game is on the line, who do you want to find? Check out www.4th-and-inches.com

*George Teague & Family First you mystified us when picked off that interception and ran it back to win the National Championship at Alabama and then again on Thanksgiving day to knock my Lions out of the playoffs when you were with Green Bay. Then you brought tears to my eyes when you *knocked Terrell Owens off of the star at Cowboys Stadium.* You never ceased to amaze me. www.GeorgeTeagueandFriends.com

*Francious Faulkner One of the top "Print-Designers & Embroiders of the Future", that's been putting it down for decades consistently since my college days. If you ever need a large amount of work done right the first time in a short amount of time look him up www.IceWorldInc.biz

*Rocky Parker Rocky came up with a nice concept for student athletes to show them proper form, competitiveness & sportsmanship. Check out www.TexasSchoolOfFootball.com ,

*Clay Mack D1-Sports Sports Complex-Dallas, TX. He is one of the top Trainers and Secondary Coaches in the Metroplex. If he can't get your footwork right, then you're in the wrong occupation.

*Coach Chris Givens Thanks for helping me when I needed it the most! My career might have been over

before it started if it wasn't for you! Thanks for the expert tutelage.

*Mechelle Williams-Ambit Energy Company; Not only can she help you to save Considerably on your Electricity Bills {Residential & Commercial} but can help you to make $ as well. Check out www.mewill.Energy526.com And start saving Today!

*Norman Sparrow owner of restaurant "The Table is Bread" in B.R., La. www.TableIsBread.net

*Tarsha Polk www.TheMarketingLady.com This lady can give you insight on bringing your business to light!

*Deborah Dillard {the President of Social Media Voice-Dialogue Management Solutions. Whenever you need to give your product or service a voice on Social Media, hit her up. www.SocialMediaVoice.net

*Coach John Montgomery {Thanks for giving me a fair-chance and an opportunity to showcase my skills. It was hard, but it was fair! One of your greatest attributes was your ability to communicate with your players and get them to visualize the task at hand. Also, that left-handed stance that you taught for OT's came in handy on the next level. I appreciate the experience.

*Coach Ralph Williams Thanks for your expert tutelage & assistance: Most of all, thanks for coming to pick me up the morning of the Nichols St. game, I

will be forever grateful & telling my Grandkids or somebody else's grandkids about you. If they had more football coaches like you that actually cared about their players as a person, instead of just what can you do for me on the field/ or what have you done for me lately, this would be a better sport, but in my own words," *It's not a nice game!*"

*Randy Manning- a former team-mate who put me up on extra "*game*" to go with the terrain when I transferred down south. He showed me how to apply my entrepreneurial skills and to network to greater heights. He stressed the importance of looking good, playing good & getting good grades to break the stereotype of the typical athlete. We weren't just 2 of the best dressed "*Big-Men*" on campus; we were 2-of the Best Dressed on campus period from head to toe.

We didn't go to the show; we were the Show & when we showed up, and we "*Showed Out!*" On the field & off! He also showed me how to apply the accounting concepts of "*Assets & Liabilities*" and "*Debits & Credits*" to real life scenarios and to take inventory of those on my personal team. Randy stressed the importance of staying focused & to "*make the money and not chase the honeys.*"

*Coach Pete Richardson- You took winning to another level! They need to name a stadium after you!

*Coach Bill Williamson and Coach Willard Bailey Anytime you are ready to start another program, hit me up! I am the man with the plan!

*Coach Jack Phillips {A former NFL Player -Chiefs/ College Coach & former teammate of mine that has a passion for the game. Best known for his relentless play as a player & a technician of the game, Jack is now getting the best out of his players as a Coach and a Trainer. He is highly regarded as a *"Master of Secondary Play."*

*Dr. Penny St. James-Entrepreneurial Business Centers of America / The St. James-Marketing Agency.

*Marlon Edwards-He got our vote for "Small Business Entrepreneur of The Year" with ***"Suave-Handyman-Mechanic & Moving Services***"-Dallas, TX. Where they bring the repairs to you! Everybody needs a Handyman!

*Dr. Krystal Barnett-Frisco, TX. This is ***one of the finest Doctors in America & she doesn't use scalpels nor needles!*** At her office they get your body tight & right plus keep your health and nutrition on point naturally without drugs or pharmaceuticals. Definitely the wave of the future! Check out www.DrKrystalBarnett.com ; www.DrKrystalExtraordinaryHealth.com and www.MaximizedLiving.com you will be glad you did!

*Joe Bean {Commissioner of the SAFL-Football League & NAACP-Regional Representative. A former teammate who always stood for what he believed in and gave 100% on the field and never quit in the face of adversity. Thanks for the hook-up! www.logoserver.com/SAFL.html

*Dr. Tray Andrews -DC. - Owner of the Lake Houston Wellness Center near Houston, TX. This is another one of the finest Doctors in America & she doesn't use scalpels nor needles either! *She is serious about her trade & her craft.* www.LakeHoustonWellness.com

*Ozell Graham at The Fade Shop-Dallas, TX www.FadeShop.com {**winners of The Chosen One Sports: "*People's Choice*" Award**. the owner-Ozell took a concept that he developed in the military and turned it into a Franchise in the civilian world. You can get your top cropped & your shoes shined at the same time! If you're ever in Dallas, TX stop through. You may be surprised as to who you may run into up in there.

*Travis Pearson {Barber in Dallas, TX. Who not only is sharp at his craft, but has the business side of the game down so good that he spends about as much time on the golf course as he does in the shop.

*Crystal-owner of Eye Candy-Waxing & Threading Brow Salon -Dallas, TX
www.EyeCandyBrowSalon.com

*Tye Diggs {He is known as "The King of Parties" Host, Singer, Song-writer & Promoter-Dallas, TX.

*Mike Chatman-Once a "Cold-Blooded" Kick-Returner & RB, now owner of Chatman Realty & Reliable Tax Returns-Dallas/Ft. Worth, TX . "Changing Real-Estate 1-Smile at a Time!" www.MichaelDChatman.Kw.realty.com and www.ReliableTaxReturnsSrv.com

*Terrance "*Abdullah*" Sanders aka "Coach-Tiny" NFL-Giants/Browns & now owner of Powerhouse Pro-Style Training-Arlington, TX. A former teammate of mine that went to almost as many colleges as I did, who is now training Champions. Legendary Hall of Fame Coach Bill Parcels gave him the name "Tiny" and it stuck with him. www.ProStyleTraining.net

*John Breen-Photography-Dallas, TX. One of the Best in Town & One of the Best Around! www.BreenPhotography.com

*BJ. Jackson {The owner of Prema Day Spa Plano, TX. "Royal Treatment at Reasonable Rates" www.PremaDaySpa.net

*Kateria Baggett aka "Lady-T" One of the hottest up & coming female radio personalities in the DFW-Metroplex! Check her out www.LadyTsaySomething.com

*Bishop Dwight Pate - founder of Church Point Ministries & WNDC-AM Radio-B.R, La. This man always has an encouraging word that's uplifting. Check out his book "I Think I Thought I Knew!!!" www.BishopDwightPate.com

*Coach Petaway-Detroit Buccaneers This was a man of principles. I apologize for getting thrown out of the Semi-final game & costing our team the chance to play in the championship. The guy had hit me with a "cheap-shot" & I retaliated. It was a lesson in Life. Since then I have learned how to control my "*Inner-Ike*" to play & (now coach) within the confines of the rules of the game. I further developed my concepts of good sportsmanship to realize that sometimes one's actions affect more than oneself and that you have to operate for the common good of the team even if it means waiting for the next play or "*taking one for the team!*"

*Coach Cunningham-Detroit Buccaneers He emphasized certain principles of manhood including the fact that a man must have a job & that a job is what's necessary! His words of wisdom helped me to stay focused and put things in proper perspective including a better outlook on life; because I was about to quit a "high-dollar" paying job that I liked to play the game that I loved.

*Coach Kelley Goodman –The former NFL-Player & Coach who helped me to develop & master my "*board-skills*" to an unbelievable level through competition and brain-storming sessions. Also, I had to borrow a couple of those good theories & techniques to pass along to my players and put in my "*pamphlet.*"

*Devin Wyman- Author, Coach, Evangelist & Former NFL/AFL Great with the Patriots, Vikings & San Jose

Saber-cats, Now doing a Great Work for The Lord and in the Community. *"Hard work pays off!"* www.TheWinningEdge.US

*Terry Glenn- Former All-American Player@ Ohio St. & NFL Star with the Patriots & Cowboys/Offensive Coordinator for the Texas Revolution –Indoor Football/Arena Championship Team 2015'. His approach to the game sets him apart from the Rest.

*Donald Campbell-*aka Bishop Don "Magic" Juan* - Author & Consultant to the stars. Stresses the importance of being true to the game & that whatever you do, *"Take GOD with You!"*

*Shay Ashford- The Ultimate Reality Shows-she came in and saw the vision and embraced it. Thank You for utilizing and encompassing a lot of my clients in your endeavors.

*Reynaldo Rey-RIP Comedian & mentor to one of my good friends.

*Torrence Williams-Photographer-Dallas, TX Has one to the Top-Modeling Portfolios in the State!

*Allison C. Tucker Jr. Best known as "The Silent Partner" is One of the Top concert & event promoters in TEXAS. Working smoothly behind the scenes, he makes things happen on a Large Scale. www.TheSilentPartner.biz

*Dr. Hank Seitz World renowned author & Business Coach who helps positively motivated sales professionals create more clients, cash and time

using a proven success formula. Check out his books "Think, Feel and Grow Rich" & "The Happiest Man In the World" and Enrich Yourself. If you need to "*fuel-inject"* your business, hit him up and tell him that we sent you! www.ThinkFeelAndGrowRich.US ; www.DrHankSeitz.com

*Big Daddie the DJ One of New Orleans finest & a popular Radio DJ in the Dallas/ Ft. Worth area. If he can't get your event cranking, you don't have one. www.bdTHEDJ.com

*BIG-D AUTOMOTIVE-Dallas, Texas. Thanks for keeping my foreign whips on "*Tight Grips*" & maintaining them at the "***Players-Price***" because *Important* things are riding on my tires and Proper Maintenance is Essential!

*Ellen Ellis- Fashion Designer & Owner of A.O.S. Sportswear & Swimwear.

*Coach Alonzo Carter-A Coach who is making a difference in the lives of young men as well as on the field in College Football.

*Chef Joseph Randall II - The CEO of Nana's Barbecue & catering in Allen, TX. Where they bring /or ship the "Q" to You! www.NanasBBQ.com First impressions are lasting impressions and I was impressed! Falls off the bone & mouth watering!

*Tudi Wilson aka '*Tudilicious"* who achieved fame on the FOX Reality show "Master Chef "-Season 2 and for her Gourmet BBQ Sauces. www.tudilicious.com

*Chef Keith Hicks & the owners Herb & Caroline of Button's Restaurant in Ft. Worth & Addison, TX. www.ButtonsRestaurant.com This is one of my favorite places in Dallas to go relax & unwind after a long week. The atmospheres & the cuisine are unmatched. Chef Keith Hick's signature dishes & The Live Bands performing simultaneously make for an unbeatable combination. Also a Great Place to Network & the Sunday Brunches are memorable.

*Corey Austin- an impact player and owner of a Waffle House franchise in Rockwall, TX. Thanks for making a difference & sponsoring the All-star Game & my youth organization. We gave the phrase "Time to Eat" a whole new meaning.

*Special Shout-Out to Lewis H. Williams III with the *"I Hustle Nation"* down in Houston, TX. www.iHustleNation.com One of the "Ultimate Hustlers" who has revolutionized the game & mapped out blueprints for success and how to win in life with his books, videos, radio-blogs & events.

*Monte Tayion Holland- former teammate of my brother's that went from Corporate Executive to a Corporate Tycoon as owner of Tayion clothing company which is in my opinion one of the smoothest & flavorful custom clothing lines around that's "so fresh & so clean". See for yourself www.Tayion.com . If you don't know, now you Know! "They put the *"ooth"* in Smooth & have *"Big-Fella"* sizes too!

*David Mott This guy has been "*Good-People*" & down since day-1. I observed how he transformed a corporate 401k into a Corporation & a tourist attraction in the "Greek-town" section of downtown Detroit, Mi. that's been in business over a decade and ships Worldwide www.GoodPeoplePopcorn.com "Where the People & the Popcorn make the Difference".

*Connie Morgan CEO-AMPS Magazine-Dallas, Texas. Whenever you need the "Amp" turned up on your business, product, service or project, consult with them www.dallas.amspmagazine.com

*Teddy Davey -The Owner of The Balcony Club {#1 Jazz Bar in Dallas. Whenever you need to relax your mind so you can concentrate or interview a prospective new client or a date, this is the place to relax & unwind. The music is pure & refreshing and the atmosphere is laid back. A lot of the top Jazz artists have passed through here. www.TheBalconyClub.com

*Coach John Carroll - President & Head Coach of the North Texas Cowboys Youth Football organization. www.ntxcowboys.org

*DeAndre Jackson Former CFL & AFL football player now turned businessman and Owner of "***Winners BBQ***" in Plano, Texas who is "*Smokin the Competition!*" With a product that separates them from the rest, they are a *Candidate* for the Chosen One Sports-"People's Choice" Award for one of the

Top Barbeque spots in town. See for yourself www.WinnersBBQ.com

*Lincoln Parks aka *"LP"* & *"Billionaire Bruce Wayne"*- The underground rapper, actor; Radio show host, model & musician who hails from Flint, Michigan transformed his career using major mainstream moves. Tired of the games people played in the entertainment industry, he went solo and kicked it off with his first album "*Black Sunday*" which was a classic and came back a few years later with the "*Bruce Wayne*" album which confirmed the status of who he is. His LIVE shows are something to see! Check him out on www.BillionaireBruceWayne.weebly.com in addition to his latest CD "Gotham City."

*Sharon Poole-The Dallas Morning News. She was referred to us for our outstanding services and she made an instant impact by inviting me to tap into her networks and associations to achieve optimal results after viewing my manuscripts. She is definitely an asset to their publication as well as the community.

*Kia Davis aka *"Kia-D"* The Dynamic Show Host & Radio Personality for www.WeTalkRadio.com

*Kevin Poole Jr. The Owner of "WE EDIT SPORTS USA" who came in the second half of the game on these books and literally put points on the board in a short amount of time. Their commercials, video

graphics & logo spins are *"Amazingly Unique."* www.WeEditSportsUSA.com

*Kisha Taylor The owner of American Soul Café & Catering –Dallas, TX where they put their *"Heart & Soul"* into Every Meal & they deliver and *"Bring the Soul to You!"* Event Planning is also a Specialty. *www.AmericanSoulCafe.com*

*Mathew Whittier -The Vice President & Co-owner of Offense-Defense camps which provides enrichment opportunities for Football Players and Coaches nationwide. www.O-D.com

*Marvin Phillips - Owner of "MARVELOUS LIMOSINES" –Detroit; where they give a Limousine Ride a whole New Feel.

*Connie Arceneaux- Owner of Phenominal Palace Salon and Mystique Lounge Houston, TX, who also happens to own a Promotions company complete with *"Street Teams".* If you're ever in the Houston market or trying to get in, hit her up to get your event, product or service to *"Blow-up!"*

*Fred Da'Barber at Lin's Barber & Beauty shop in Friso, TX. This is the spot where you can get a Fresh cut and a good dose of knowledge & Current events at the same time.

*Dr. Jen Welter aka "Coach Jen" {She is formerly one of the top female athletes in the world & the first to play & Coach professional football with men, now working as a sports psychologist and trainer to the

stars. If you need motivation, inspiration or encouragement or if your mind or your game needs strengthening, look her up: www.JenWelter.com *"If you want to Win, put Coach Jen In!"*

*Brian Pearson -Service Manager at the Brakes Plus in Frisco, Texas. All I can say is that when you drive a Benz {or any other high-end vehicle) & you're trying to win or make ends, you need a friend on your team that specializes in keeping you rolling at the player's price or team rate! Proper maintenance is essential, and when they go down, you still need to get around. Just like in the "Pros" *you can't make the club in the tub"*, **it's hard to make a cent if you're not at the event!** www.brakesplus.com

*Kyle Whitley with Whitley Ink & Whitley Inc.

*Bro. Gilbert Melendez www.DallasTicketsUSA.com owner of one of the top Ticket Brokerages in the Dallas/ Ft. Worth area who gives back to the community with his weekly Bible-studies and feeding of the homeless & hungry both spiritually & literally. If you ever need tickets to any major sporting event or entertainment activity, spend your money where you know your seed is going to be multiplied and uplift the community at the same time.

*Tommy Benizio - Former Commissioner of the IFL & CEO of the Texas Revolution-Arena Football team. www.TexasRevs.com I want to thank you for allowing me to come in and apply some of the principles in my books to help motivate & inspire the

team to overcome adversity, deaths and injuries to achieve greatness by reaching the Championship.

*Bruce Badgett- Owner of Champions Edge Energy Sports Drink www.GetChampionsEdge.com & part owner of The Dallas Sidekicks –Professional Indoor Soccer Team www.DallasSidekicks.com . While we were on the road to success & the Championship, we were sipping on *"Bruce-Juice"* aka-*"Champions Edge Energy Sports Drink."*

*DeForest Hart- Director of America's Next Draft Pick Reality Show. www.AmericasNextDraftPick.com

*Darius Fudge All-star Arena Football Player & Accountant with SMD Consulting & Accounting who not only put up good numbers on the field, but can help you to accumulate good numbers on your financial statement and in your bank account! www.SMDaccounting.com

*Carlandre Bussey Former Champion Football Player now manager of *"The Inspiration Band"* which when they perform, it's not just a show, but an *Experience!* www.InspirationBand.com

*Candace "Mahogany" Miller aka "Mahogany the Artist" Musician/ Instructor, Band Director; Contemporary Jazz Artist & Praise Team Leader who is multi-faceted versatile and extremely talented. She not only shares the knowledge of her gifts through a program and Music School that she developed called *"Jazz BeCuzz"*, she practices what she preach and gives back as a Praise Team Leader at a Major Church in North Dallas. Experience the many facets of her endeavors: www.jazzbecuzzac.com ; www.mahoganytheartist.com ; https://candacemahoganymiller.bandcamp.com/releases

*Herschel Walker- The former Olympian & Heisman Trophy Winner from Georgia and ALL-PRO/NFL-HOF with the Dallas Cowboys & Vikings who inspired me with his work ethic and humble-down to earth attitude as a young athlete and later in Life after meeting him. Herschel set precedence in football by being one of the first to bring in a Multi-Million Dollar contract in the USFL with the New Jersey Generals. Now as Entrepreneur he is making more moves than on the field. Like him on Facebook: Famous34 ,in addition to checking out Herschel Walker's "Renaissance Man Food Services" supplying quality foods across America. http://www.renmanfoods.com

*Tim Brown- The Heisman Trophy Winner from Notre Dame & NFL-HOF Great from the Oakland Raiders. Now GM/owner of the Texas Revolution-Arena Football team.

*Jameis Winston-The Heisman Trophy Winner, Watkins Award Winner and National Champion from Florida State who was also first round draft pick of the Tampa Bay Buccaneers.

*Vincent "V.C." Castile -aka "*The Celebrity Barber*" in Dallas, Texas. Making the World Famous one cut at a time, he is best known in the Hair-Game for innovative promotions & for having more Celebrities & Professional Athletes as clients than the next 2-contenders combined. Check out his website www.CelebrityBarber.com and get a clue as to what's really going on.

*Jeff Davis {More than just a "*World Class Barber*" but an upper echelon experience. The concept and atmosphere that he provides not only allows you to relax your mind so that you can concentrate, but treat yourself to an "in-town" get away. Look up www.WorldClassBarber.com and www.AstuteGentlemen.com I was Impressed.

*Lawrence Mann A Mann of many talents! Owner of the Top Achievers Training Program and the Director of the Mann Up Program for Plano, Schools. He is known as one of the Top Basketball Recruiters and AAU-Coaches in North Texas. One of his specialties is Photography & Graphic Art which brings photos to life. Check out www.TopAchieversPlano.org & www.LawrenceMannPhotography.com

*Aerosmith- shout-out to all the guys in the band who supported us in our efforts. www.AerosmithTribute.com

*Earl Lloyd-RIP -The father of one of my good friends Kevin and the First African-American Player & Coach in the NBA. He paved the way and helped to create many opportunities for others through his

hard work and perseverance. His legacy lives on & will soon have a postal stamp with his image. Pick up his book: "Moon Fixer" available on www.Amazon.com and in major bookstores.

*Arthur Muhammad - Owner/Film Director & Producer of the movie "CARTER HIGH". We are thankful that he has allowed us to participate in the movie and to help promote it Nationwide to bring insight to players on all levels. He overcame insurmountable odds to fund & film this movie which will be a staple in every football lover's movie catalog & collection. This is a Prime Example of how "You can Win if You Don't Quit!" Check it out www.TheCarterHighMovie.com and his other works www.SweetChariotFilms.com , https://pro-labs.imdb.com/name/nm2584377

**Dr. George C. Fraser This man was a guest on one of our Radio shows and blew our mind in a short period of time. He runs the* "Power Networking Conference" and *opened our eyes to some alarming facts to make us more aware of our surroundings and those we surround ourselves with. "If your 5-Closest Friends aren't worth at least $500,000 collectively, then you have a lot of work to do!" "67% of most people that graduate from college never open or read another book in their life." He not only laced us up with information on how to Successfully multiply your seeds to achieve generational wealth and empower your offspring for the next two generations to come, but plugged us into his concept of "Learn, Earn & Return". For more* *knowledge that they don't teach in College, check out www.FraserNet.com*

*Jerry Jones owner of the Dallas Cowboys-NFL www.DallasCowboys.com Check out his book "***PLAYING TO WIN.***"*

**The other Big-Ray- Entrepreneur/ part owner of the Allen Arena Football team & Big-Ray's BBQ-Allen, TX. www.BigRaysBarbeque.com if you're ever in town, come around and ask for the "Big Ray Special"! *"We have that flavor that you savor & a price that's nice!"*

Special Note:

With $uccess in Life being a Team-Effort, you are going to need as many avenues as you can get to promote your product, service, theme or cause in the guise of Branding/Marketing and Name Recognition. It's a numbers game. In order to achieve your goal, you will need a certain number/quantity and quality of people to subscribe to your theory, products or services. Feel free to utilize or contact some of the aforementioned resources if you have a "Need" that needs to be supplied within their area of expertise and ***don't forget to ask for "The Big-Ray $pecial!"*** *You may be surprised as to what the power of divine connections can do for you and yours.*

*We give **Thanks and Glory to GOD** for allowing us to have this network, associations & divine connections. We would also like to thank all of the Scouts, Recruiters, Players, Coaches, Camp-Directors and CHAMPIONS that came through Chosen One Sports www.Chosen1Sports.com & the Supports Staff for all of their assistance and patronage. *"Many were called, few were Chosen..."* **CHAMPIONS ALWAYS FIND A WAY TO WIN!** With you we achieved Extraordinary RESULTS! "Greatness is not a Coincidence"! Together-Everybody-Achieves-More! If you ever have a Sports Related product, movie, event or concept that you need marketed, promoted or introduced into diverse target markets or need Sports figures/ actors to appear in movie premiers, *hit them up at* (972)CHOSEN-1

**Last but not the least, we would like to thank everybody on the TEAM at www.BigRayInternational.com where "Winning is a Lifestyle"-Embrace It! Their hard work and dedication paid off.

If ***You Need Connections, Contacts & Information*** to have a Book, Event, Radio Talk-show, product, service or concept that you developed marketed, promoted & introduced into diverse target markets. Hit them up online, email: PromoteYourself@BigRayInternational.com or CALL on the "*Big-Ray International*" *hotline*.

"We can have your phone Blowing up like a Volcano"

"Sometimes it's not the amount of times that you try, but more-so the means by which one is willing to go through to achieve their objective!"

***WARNING!* PLEASE DO NOT LOAN YOUR BOOK *"WINOLOGY: The 48-Laws of Winning"* OUT! YOU MAY NEVER GET IT BACK! or worse, your main competition may get their hands on it & retaliate for years of frustration!**

The Bottom Line: **"WE GET RESULTS!"**

www.MillionDollarSideHustle.com

www.Chosen1Sports.com

www.BigRayInternational.com

www.48LawsOfWinning.com

www.WinningIsALifestyle.com

Made in the USA
Coppell, TX
30 December 2023